MW00946797

Corporate Travel
Hiding in Plain Sight

Claudia Unger

Copyright © Claudia Unger 2016

The right of Claudia Unger to be identified as the author
of this work has been asserted by her in accordance
with the Copyright, Designs and Patents Act 1988.

All rights reserved. No part of this publication may be
reproduced, stored in a retrieval system or transmitted in any form or by any means (electronic, mechani-
cal, photocopying, recording or otherwise), without the
prior written permission of the author.

Editorial & Design Services: The Write Factor
www.thewritefactor.co.uk

Corporate Travel
Hiding in Plain Sight

Corporate Travel
Hiding in Plain Sight

Claudia Unger

Table of Contents

2. Corporate Travel: Past, Present, and Future 43

3. Who is Who in Corporate Travel 81

4. The Travel Program 123

5. The Trip Life Cycle   155

Table of Figures

Acknowledgements

There are many people without whom this book wouldn't have been possible. First of all, thanks to my dad, Manfred Unger, who read the early drafts before it went to the editor. Secondly, I'm very thankful to my editor Lorna Howarth for all the hard work and advice she's given me, making this book the best it can be.

Along the road of writing this book, many people influenced me directly and indirectly. And so I'm thanking: Hanne Unger, Julia Unger-Che, Kevin Che, Torsten Kriedt, Nicolas Dahbi, Cecile Soulier, Mike Eggleton, Jaume Bellaescusa-Mansilla, Elise Coker, Kelly Flynn, Thad Slaton, Kathy Jackson, and all my other amazing colleagues at BCD Travel; Greeley Koch, Anja Turner, Caroline Allen, Amon Cohen, Scott Torrey, David Meyer, Anja Turner, Kunal Bharti, Dr. Alan Fyall, Dr. Ian Yeoman, Peter Hyson, Hilary Rowland, Poppy Hughes, Catherine Ellis-Robson, Michael O'Keeffe, Joseph Nagle, the McInelly family, and many others who helped me stay motivated and believe in the idea.

More broadly, I'd like to thank all the media outlets and suppliers who share valuable information and research in the public domain. Without you, this book couldn't have been written.

With thanks and gratitude,

Claudia Unger

Preface

Corporate travel has been in a state of constant evolution for decades. But the speed of change now is so rapid that even those of us living through the transformation are a bit awestruck when we step back and consider just how far the industry has come. That's why Corporate Travel: Hiding in Plain Sight is so critical—and long overdue. This book documents our industry's metamorphosis and looks ahead to what's next. It's an invaluable resource for educating the talent our industry will need to grow.

This book is essential because it focuses not only on evolutionary technologies, but also—especially—on how people in our industry are adapting to change and pushing for the next wave of improvements. At BCD Travel, we pride ourselves on top-notch technology, but we know that our people make the difference. The talent, experience and entrepreneurial mindset of our employees is what keeps clients satisfied and ensures we have the strategic flexibility and adaptability to thrive amid extraordinary change.

We want to hire the best talent out there, and we'd like those new employees to have a working knowledge of the industry on day one. But that has been a challenge—so much so, that we've created our own training programs, internships and apprenticeships to make up for what's lacking in the education available to people who want to build a career in corporate travel. This book goes a long way toward filling those gaps. If it's used in a learning environment—whether that's a university classroom or an intensive industry-backed course—it can give novices the jumpstart they need to succeed in our complex, ever-changing and fascinating industry.

John Snyder, President and Chief Executive Officer, BCD Travel

Foreword

Think of a super-cool new tool tech demonstration by, let's say, Apple: you see all the amazing stuff that is now going to be possible, you find out how things relate to one another, and how you might benefit from knowing these insights. But you won't know all the details and work going on in the background.

This book is something of a tech-demo: it aims to give you an overview and introduction of the corporate travel industry. It approaches the topic from a bird's eye perspective, thus leaving out the nitty-gritty things that are important in the day-to-day work.

Having said that, the book does revolve around the work of the travel manager. It's with their jobs in mind that the structure and outline was decided upon. Mainly, because so many people struggle to explain what it is we actually do in this industry – and that's not only to family and friends but, more importantly, to the CEOs and CFOs of the corporations the travel managers report to.

Before you dive into this book, let me give you a word of warning: there's a lot of information; there's a lot of connections and overlap between the various subjects and if ever you wanted to work in this industry, be aware that there's a lot of job diversity – and quite a bit of juggling – to do. But that aside, there's so much to gain as well; knowledge and understanding of business and economics, perks of the travel industry, the ability to move through various departments (from sales to tech support) just within corporate travel and, possibly most importantly, the people you meet along the way.

While reading, you'll come across different sources, mostly websites, and little academic material. You'll notice that BCD Travel is quoted more often than others. That's partly because they're one of the top three travel-management companies out there, partly because I used to work for them and partly because many of the white papers have been written by me.

The white papers are a great resource for anyone wanting to deepen their understanding on any of the issues discussed in this book (and there are many other companies that have very good papers publicly available). Organisations like ACTE and GBTA offer further information and education about deep-diving into the travel programme and how to conduct negotiations. And aside from the white papers, travel management companies also have a wealth of knowledge that travel managers should tap into.

But in my opinion you can't teach someone about the forest by just looking at individual trees; in other words, you need the bird's-eye view to be able to connect all the dots together. And that's the aim of this book.

With that said, I hope you find this an enjoyable, interesting and knowledge-enhancing read.

Claudia Unger

CHAPTER 1
Part of the Big Picture

By the end of this chapter you'll be able to:

✓ Define tourism and understand the big picture.

✓ Define corporate travel and explain its importance to the global economy.

✓ Know the differences between corporate travel and meetings, conferences and incentives.

✓ Have an understanding of how important corporate travel is within tourism and the global economy.

Quick Facts

* In the UK, 76 universities offer a total of 450 degrees in tourism – none of which offer corporate (or business) travel in its curriculum.

* One out of 11 jobs can be traced to tourism worldwide and the sector support 9% of the global GDP (gross domestic product).

* Academics divide business travel into four categories:
  > Meetings
  > Conferences / Exhibitions / Events
  > Incentives
  > Individual business travel (i.e. corporate travel)

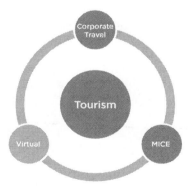

* In 2014, more than $3.2 billion was spent by just 10 companies for air bookings in the US alone. (All figures in this book are quoted in US dollars.)

Introduction

Tourism: we immediately think of sunbathing on beaches, surfing waves or skiing mountains. Recreation, relaxation and faraway places. And as nice as that is, there's another side to tourism: economics. Travel and tourism are an important contributor to national GDPs (gross domestic product), accounting for about 9% (direct, indirect and induced) globally.

There are currently 76 universities in the UK alone who offer a total of 450 tourism degrees (whatuni.com, 2015) – giving dues to the importance of the sector. However, one important part of the tourism picture is currently missing on the curriculum: corporate travel.

Traditionally, academics divide business travel into four categories: meetings, incentives, conferences and events. It's only been in the last 20 years that another category has been noted: corporate travel (i.e. individual business travel). In their book *Business Travel*, Davidson and Cope (2003) give insights into all these categories and their connections.

But now it's time to make corporate travel more accessible to a wider audience, because its economic impact is significant, and skilled people are needed to help bring this industry forward. Looking at the World Travel & Tourism Council's league tables shows the US alone as spending over $200 billion on business travel – about 1/3 of leisure spending in 2014 (WTTC, 2015).

While credit is due to Davidson and Cope for bringing this topic into the open, a single chapter on corporate travel cannot convey the complexities of this industry. To set the scene, let's look at the big picture of tourism: its impact on the global economy and the forecast of how this sector might develop in the future.

After this big-picture approach, let's zoom in closer to corporate travel. Looking at definitions and at the management side of this industry, we will then aim to find out its global significance.

Business travel is next, to give some context for corporate travel. Looking first at definitions of this, often–called MICE sector (meetings, incentives, conferences and events), we will then discuss the differences and similarities within business travel. Wonder how the MICE sector is doing and has done through the recession? Take a look at the snapshot part of this chapter to find out about the current situation, followed by trends in the industry.

Corporate travel throughout this book is used to describe individual professionals travelling for business – including those working for governments and in universities.

Business travel is used as an umbrella term for all business-related travel, including corporate travel, meetings, conferences (including events) and incentives.

Finally, we'll take a look at virtual meetings. While part of the MICE industry, they're also part of corporate travel – virtual collaboration is possibly the next big thing (though it can't make travel quite redundant just yet). Marvel at the trends: crowd–sourcing and, believe it or not, holographic meetings.

The Big Picture: Tourism

The importance of tourism for the global economy is proven beyond doubt. Organisations like the World Tourism Organisation (UNWTO) and the World Travel & Tourism Council (WTTC) are at the forefront of promoting its importance as well as educating the public of its possibilities.

And here's the proof: one in 11 jobs are supported by tourism either directly or indirectly, and the international tourism receipts totalled $1.245 billion in 2014 (UNWTO, 2015).

The Definition of Tourism

Before getting our teeth into the world of corporate travel, let's first look at some definitions of tourism. The World Tourism Organization's (UNWTO, 2014) latest definition states:

> *'Tourism is a social, cultural and economic phenomenon which entails the movement of people to countries or places outside their usual environment for personal or business/ professional purposes.'*

Another definition comes from John Tribe, who, in his book The Economics of Recreation, Leisure and Tourism (2011) writes:

> *'Tourism: Visiting for at least one night for leisure and holiday, business and professional or other tourism purposes. [Whereby] visiting means a temporary movement to destinations outside the normal home and workplace.'*

This suggests that all people travelling for business are also tourists.

Yet, they're not the holidaymakers we generally think of when hearing the term tourist. These are men and women travelling to a location with the purpose of doing business rather than to relax – although in recent years, more and more corporate travellers combine business with leisure, but more of that later.

Figure 1 is a quick guide to the differences between leisure and business travel based on the 5–W questions:

	LEISURE	BUSINESS TRAVEL
Who travels and who pays?	The traveller does both.	The employee travels, but the company pays.
Where do they go?	Destination chosen by the traveller; often coastal, mountain, rural or urban.	Destination chosen by business need i.e. location of an office or conference location.
When do they go?	The time of travel is based on their time off from work.	Dictated by business needs.
Why do they go?	Mainly to relax and take a break from work or to learn something.	To do business; could be sales, retention, relationship management but also research, product development and education.
How do they plan & book?	Traveller plans (possibly together with others who are joining) and books what seems the best offer.	Traveller plans and searches either on online booking tool or by phoning an agent; restrictions are in place as to what the traveller can select and book.

Figure 1 - Difference Between Leisure and Business Travel

Tourism Today: Impact on the Global Economy

The tourism industry, globally, contributed $6.99 billion in total to the GDP in 2013. This is forecast to increase to $10.965 billion by 2024, according to the *Travel & Tourism Economic Report* for 2014 published by the WTTC (2015). The same report also states that travel and tourism directly supported nearly 200 million jobs in 2013 worldwide.

On jobs, the World Tourism Organisation (UNWTO) states that one in 11 jobs globally can be traced to tourism (direct, indirect or induced) (UNWTO Tourism Highlights, 2015). The graphic below gives a fascinating at-a-glance overview of how vast this industry is – and thereby, how important it is for the whole world.

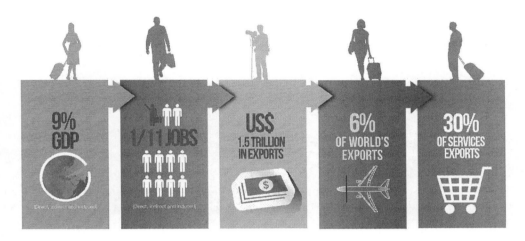

Figure 2 - Why Tourism Matters

Another graphic from the same report showcases the international tourist arrivals (ITA) and the international tourism receipts (ITR) across the globe.

Global ITA = 1,133 million
Global ITR = $1,245 billion

These are actual figures from 2014, and the forecast looks promising for the industry to continue to grow.

Figure 3 - ITA and ITR

Tourism Tomorrow: Forecast Figures

Jobs are forecast to rise by 2% per year to 126,257,000 jobs by 2024 (WTTC, 2015) for direct employment in tourism. However, looking at tourism's total contribution to global employment, the forecast figure jumps to 346,901,000 jobs. This is estimated to be 10.2% of total employment across the world.

Let's quickly clarify the terms direct, indirect and induced contribution:

With that out of the way, take a look at the below graphical illustration of total contribution of travel and tourism (T&T) to employment, reproduced from the WTTC's report referenced above.

Direct	Direct spend of residents and visitors on travel and tourism (T&T) services like accommodation, transportation, entertainment and attractions.
Indirect	Investments by providers of above-mentioned services, as well as total T&T spend by governments.
Induced	Money spent by those employed in T&T; for example, for housing and recreation.

For example, as shown previously, indirect contribution would be a percentage of those working on T&T-related investments and those working in government. The induced contribution relates to those jobs that are supported by the spending of those directly and indirectly employed in travel and tourism.

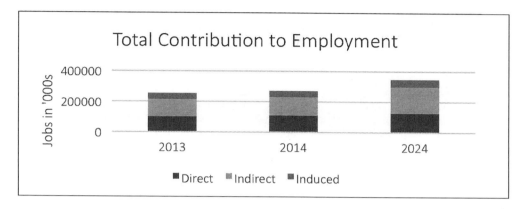

Figure 4 - Travel & Tourism Contribution

Corporate Travel, Management & the Global Economy

Corporate travel is an important part of the big picture of tourism – not only business travel. While thinking of an individual traveller going abroad for business might not sound exciting or complicated, the sheer mass of individuals travelling for their (i.e. one) company shows a different picture.

Enter corporate travel management. Saving opportunities, administration, country regulations, operations, risk management and communications are just a small part of what's going on in the back–office to get travellers safely to their destinations (and back).

And if that hasn't convinced you that this is an industry in its own right, consider that IBM in the U.S. alone spend $590 million just on air transactions in 2013. And that total business–travel spend in the US was $280.2 billion in 2014.

Corporate Travel: A Definition

So what is corporate travel? Everyone naturally has the answer to that – because the clue is in the name. Yet, that's also the most likely reason why it's gone unnoticed for so long: it's been hiding in plain sight.

Ask someone working within the industry and you're probably going to find that they have a hard time explaining what it is they do exactly. It's because when an individual person travels, the complexities and back–office procedures to get them on the road are invisible.

As stated in the introduction of this chapter, the term 'corporate travel' is used throughout this book to talk about individual business travel; whereby this includes travellers from universities and governments, i.e. non–corporates.

As Davidson and Cope (2003) state:

> *'Individual business travel refers to any trip away from the traveller's normal workplace undertaken in the course of doing his or her job. It's often referred to as Corporate Travel, even though travel may be undertaken also on behalf of other organisations, such as governments and universities.'*

Before deep–diving into the complexities of managing corporate travel, let's take a look at who might be a corporate traveller. The usual examples in text books or articles are journalists and talent–spotters; and while they certainly are corporate travellers, they're as certainly not the majority of this segment.

Who do you know who travels for business? I'm sure, when you look around at your family, friends and acquaintances you can come up with quite a number of people you know who travel for business. The most common reasons are sales and business development. People travelling for these departments are also often called 'Road Warriors' because the main part of their work is done on the road.

And even though the traveller is going to meet someone, and is possibly even accompanied by a colleague, this travel is clearly different from business travel meetings, as we'll see later in this chapter.

Other reasons employees travel are:

- **Account management**: it's after all important to maintain the relationship with face-to-face contact once in a while.

- **Special skills**: if the person has special knowledge or skill set they're often travelling to various office locations around the globe to help out.

    - A sub-group of this can be found in the oil and maritime industry; although travel is generally arranged for groups, these are all corporate travellers who are needed for special projects, usually in more or less remote locations.

- **Conference attendees**: definitely part of business travel (which is explained in more detail later). However, travellers largely book their travel through their own corporate travel department.

- **One-off travel**: this last group of employees travels at irregular intervals and for different reasons, like team meetings, speaking engagements, education and knowledge transfer.

These are all very diverse reasons for travelling, and remember it's not an exclusive list! And while it is straightforward to just go online and book your flight, train, car rental and hotel, there's much more to corporate travel than the individual making a reservation.

Corporate Travel Management

That's where corporate travel management (CTM) comes in. As you might know, corporations, governments and universities, as well as non-governmental organisations (NGOs), are bound by duty-of-care laws. They need to make sure their employees are taken care of during working hours – and when an employee travels for the company, they're doing so on company time.

This is one of the reasons why companies employ corporate travel managers, who look after the needs of travelling employees as well as the needs of the company's bottom line. We'll look more closely at their job profile in chapters three and four, but for now you need to know that their tasks include:

- Setting up a travel programme

- Creating and maintaining travel policy
- Managing daily operations
- Communicating with various stakeholders

At a glance you notice there's no mention of travel bookings – and that's rarely a travel manager's task (though it's dependent on the size of the company). And while you might think these are fairly easy tasks, remember that this is a high level overview and there's a lot more to actually do than 'just' the list.

In essence, corporate travel management is a strategic function within a company to conform to duty-of-care standards, establish compliance to travel policy, and administer the travel programme (including supplier negotiations, operations, communication, reporting, travel risk management and expense management).

In chapter three, the travel manager role is discussed in detail and the travel management company (TMC) is introduced. In short, they're helping the travel manager cope with their annual, quarterly, monthly, weekly and daily tasks.

Corporate Travel and the Global Economy

Corporate travel contributes to the global economy and the jury is still out as to which comes first – essentially, it's a chicken and egg story.

1   Does corporate travel lead the economy?

     Companies explore investment opportunities in times of economic downturn and thus increase expenditure. This, in turn, has a positive effect on the economy (either of that particular country or even on a global level).

2   Does the economy lead corporate travel?

     When the economy is up, companies increase their sales efforts to make the most of the current situation.

Either way you look at it, it's a fact that the two are closely linked together.

The WTTC publishes league tables of spend by category, business travel among them (2015). The 10 highest spending countries collectively spent over $804.5 billion in 2014. It's perhaps unsurprising that most of these countries are found in the so-called first world, China and Malaysia being the exceptions.

Rank	Country	$ in billion
1	United States of America	280.2
2	China	142.6
3	United Kingdom	98.5
4	Germany	79.8
5	Japan	75.7
6	France	38.5
7	Italy	29.3
8	Sweden	20.2
9	Malaysia	20.1
10	Canada	19.6

And this list of countries is going to remain relatively static when looking at the forecast for 2025.

Rank	Country	$ in billion
1	United States of America	373.3
2	China	247.9
3	United Kingdom	133.5
4	Germany	100.7
5	Japan	91.4
6	France	45.2
7	India	36.1
8	Malaysia	36.0
9	Italy	32.2
10	Sweden	29.2

India is the only 'new country' that makes the league in 2025, while many European countries slow business–travel spend. Still, with an accumulated $1,125.5 billion forecasted spend, corporate travel is growing and gaining importance. Especially as trade treaties are being drafted and are in place already.

In relative terms, based on percentage of GDP, the WTTC's list changes substantially. It shows the importance of corporate travel to emerging economies, particularly in Africa. Only Malaysia is part of both tables.

Rank	Country	% total of GDP
1	Seychelles	5.0
2	Lesotho	4.9
3	Mauritius	4.8
4	Tonga	4.6
5	Mali	3.4
6	Kiribati	3.0
7	Malaysia	2.9
8	Honduras	2.9
9	Malawi	2.6
10	Senegal	2.5

And finally, the last table is on those countries that grew fastest in 2014 in terms of business-travel spend. None of these countries has made it on the big spender list as yet, however.

Rank	Country	Real growth, %
1	Armenia	27.0
2	Sri Lanka	20.2
3	Qatar	19.5
4	Iceland	18.7
5	Albania	14.8
6	Iraq	14.7
7	Myanmar	13.4
8	Nepal	13.1
9	Aruba	11.9
10	Indonesia	11.6

As a reminder in statistics: if there's very little business–travel spend in a country currently and this is doubled, it's still quite a small amount. Please bear this in mind when looking at these tables; full details and projections of the business travel league tables can be found on the WTTC website.

The WTTC defines business–travel spend as 'spending on business travel within a country by residents and international visitors' (2015). This seems in line with corporate travel figures: the annual sales turnover of the three biggest travel management companies is approximately $85 billion.

Another source backing these findings is the Corporate Travel 100 list, published by Business Travel News (BTN 2014). This is looking at air spend in the USA only; although some companies share data of their global air spend, US overall travel and entertainment (T&E) spend and global overall T&E spend. Leading the list is IBM with $590 million; and the combined air spend of the top 10 companies is $3.2 billion.

In the following chapters, corporate travel is looked at in much more detail. But rather than focussing on spend figures and global importance, it's the history, stakeholders, processes and finally even the individual traveller that we're going to hone in on.

However, meetings, incentives, conferences and events are important parts of business travel, too! So before delving more into the world of corporate travel, let's have a look at these and see how they connect. There's also information on key differentiators so that you're in the know of what's what.

MICE – Meetings, Incentives, Conferences & Events

On the following pages we're going to look at MICE, a standard acronym for Meetings, Incentives, Conferences and Events. All of which are forms of business travel and therefore lend themselves for discussion to better understand the context of corporate travel. Please note that there's some debate whether the 'E' stands for events or exhibitions; for the purpose of this book exhibitions are included under the conference umbrella, whereas events are a separate category.

It also has to be noted that there are a number of people in the industry who feel that the word MICE doesn't reflect the importance (or economic scale) properly. Hence the words 'Meetings and Events' or just 'Meetings Industry' are now much more commonly used.

However, hit by the economic downturn of 2008, the meetings industry suffered a lot of cancellations and subsequent budget cuts – giving concern to its economic scalability after all. Yet in 2014, this started to truly turn around with budget increases for meetings, rising demand and, naturally, higher rates. But budgets are still being tightly monitored and controlled, and this is discussed in more detail (including what's going on in the industry today – and what is likely to come tomorrow) later in this section.

MICE – A Definition

Let's look at the MICE components in a bit more detail, ranking them by participant numbers.

Incentives	An employee (usually together with other employees of the company) is rewarded with a trip for excellent performance.
Meetings	Start from just two people coming together for a discussion. Usually, in the business travel context, it's 10 people and upward.
Events	Taking a client (or potential client) to prestigious or cultural events like a World Cup, Wimbledon or the Glyndebourne opera festival.
Conferences	Tens to thousands of participants coming together mainly for educational purposes, trade shows and exhibitions.

And by scrabbling the initials this way you now know how IMEX (no, not the cinema!) came to its name; though they replaced conferences for exhibitions.

As stated before, there's some debate about the naming of this sector. Therefore, when you're looking for MICE in the WTO glossary, it redirects you to meetings industry. Their working definition is:

> *'To highlight purposes relevant to the meetings industry, if a trip's main purpose is business/professional, it can be further subdivided into "attending meetings, conferences or congresses, trade fairs and exhibitions" and "other business and professional purposes".*
>
> *The term meetings industry is preferred by the International Congress and Convention Association (ICCA), Meeting Professionals International (MPI) and Reed Travel over the acronym MICE (Meetings, Incentives, Conferences and Exhibitions) which does not recognize the industrial nature of such activities.'*

Let's now look at how some other organisations explain MICE, starting with the International Congress and Convention Association (ICCA 2013). They favour the word 'exhibitions' over 'events':

__Meeting__ general term indicating the coming together of a number of people in one place, to confer or carry out a particular activity. Frequency: can be on an ad hoc basis or according to a set pattern, as for instance annual general meetings, committee meetings, etc.

__Incentive__ meeting event as part of a programme which is offered to its participants to reward a previous performance.

__Conference__ participatory meeting designed for discussion, fact-finding, problem-solving and consultation. As compared with a congress, a conference is normally smaller in scale and more select in character – features which tend to facilitate the exchange of information. The term "conference" carries no special connotation as to frequency. Though not inherently limited in time, conferences are usually of limited duration with specific objectives.

__Exhibition__ Events at which products and services are displayed.

Recently, there has been an industry driven initiative to not use the "MICE Market" label and instead say "The Meetings Industry", which encompasses all the above.'

With the last sentence there's yet another way to describe this industry introduced. Just note that there are many terms out there – and they seem to be changing quite quickly.

IMEX, also called IMEX-Frankfurt, is one of the most important exhibitions for the MICE sector. With their hosted buyer programme (buyers have all expenses paid) they attract a large number of exhibitors, customers and other stakeholders to their annual show.

In 2010 IMEX-America was launched – the same format, but held in Las Vegas.

MICE & Corporate Travel

Now that you have a better understanding of the meetings side of business travel, let's look at how MICE and Corporate Travel are related – and different.

Remember figure one? It outlines the key differences between leisure and business travel. And you noticed there's no further differentiation between business and corporate travel. That's because there are two ways to look at the meetings sector:

- As a meetings organiser
- As a meetings participant

So to avoid confusion, we'll be using the word 'meetings' for the following discussion as it applies to all MICE business travel – and is easier to compare with corporate travel.

As a meetings organiser you're responsible for the overall event. You decide on the location, book the venue, contact speakers, arrange exhibition stands, block guest rooms (possibly at a preferable rate), and send out invites to your participants. There's a whole industry around all the above, which only gives you a small insight into all that's going on behind the scene and before the meeting.

However, what the meeting organiser doesn't do (and we're talking here about the norm rather than the exception) is arrange travel for the participants. So we're back to square one: corporate travel.

As an employee in a company, you might very well want to participate in a conference that is closely linked to your daily work. You approach your manager for trip approval (more of that later) and then contact your travel department, giving them the necessary details to book your trip. They MIGHT ask you to book the hotel through the meeting's organiser, but very often they'll book a hotel that is part of the corporate travel programme (more of that later too).

Hence the two are very much connected, and no corporate travel is ever done completely in isolation (unless a company deals in asceticism and sends their employees on cave days). The real difference is the focus; either on the traveller (i.e. corporate travel) or on the meeting (i.e. MICE).

MICE – A Snapshot

The meetings industry, like so many others, was hit hard by the recession. With demand falling steadily from 2008 onwards, hotels (and other venues) were unable to increase rates. In short: it was a buyers' market – and we'll come back to this in the next chapter.

However, a survey by Business Travel News (BTN) in 2014 showed that MICE is back on track (Beauchamp 2014). Not only did meeting budgets increase (and still do), but there's more demand for incentives as well. And that's where you have another indicator for how the economy is doing. Companies are sharing their good fortunes to increase employee motivation, which suffered during the years of tighter budget controls.

Going back to their article, BTN 'reported 39 percent of respondents indicated their organisations' 2013 meetings expenditure increased from 2012, and 40 percent predicted another year–over–year increase in 2014'.

In their Industry Forecast 2015 published in September 2014, Advito (a business travel consultancy) stated that meeting spend is on the mend (Advito, 2014). Due to a lack of new capacity coming into the market in 2015 – especially in core business travel destinations – rates are increasing. It also pointed to shorter lead times: if you want to organise a meeting, you better plan ahead as popular venues are booked at least six months in advance.

While business is returning and more meetings are planned and in the pipeline, buyers are still cautious about budgets. This shows mainly in entertainment and food and beverage budgets. The term 'no frills', which is widely used in the airline business, has found its way into the meeting industry. When before it was common to book an all–inclusive package, usually containing audio/visual equipment, room hire, coffee breaks and (some) meals, it's now much more common to hire the venue and select everything else based on budget. This means hotels and other venues had to adjust their catering options quite drastically to meet the new demands.

Trends in MICE

As discussed, the industry is finding its foothold back and spending is on the increase, albeit with a cautious mind. Let's now look at some of the emerging trends in this industry that are closely related to corporate travel.

Integrating Travel and Meetings (ITM)

This is still quite a new trend, whereby companies are getting smarter with their overall travel and meeting spending.

In the past, different departments dealt with corporate travel and meetings, usually without much interaction. When the belts were tightened, however, and new ways of savings were being sought, an opportunity was found in bringing those two closer together.

A first step to successful ITM is to implement strategic meeting management (SMM) into the meetings programme. This basically means to stick with one or two suppliers for meetings in order to get better deals (as a trade–off for more business).

As discussed later in this book, it's common in corporate travel to negotiate rates with a variety of suppliers, including hotels. The trend with ITM is to combine the buying power, thereby ensuring better rates for the company as a whole.

Office Space Rentals – by Hotels

In recent years, and especially with the emergence of the sharing economy, hotels have been looking into new ways to rent their meeting rooms, even on an hourly basis (Botsman, 2014).

For corporate travellers there's always the question where to work while abroad. It just happens that there's time between seeing different clients or travel has been arranged early to ensure time for preparing a presentation.

While most hotels offer a desk in the room, it's often not the preferred choice for the traveller – especially when on a multi-day (or week) trip.

Hotels have seen this niche and are now offering their meeting rooms as offices for anyone who needs it. They can be rented by the hour or for a full day (or even longer), making these spaces usable when they're not let for a conference.

One big benefit that is emerging for the traveller is that meetings can be conducted in this space as well. Before they often had to go to a coffee shop or restaurant, or (much worse) to the hotel room.

Hybrid Meetings

These are a cross between real and virtual meetings, and we're talking about virtual meetings in the next section in more detail.

Basically, it's a way to facilitate a face-to-face meeting for those living within a certain area and to use video-conferencing to share the meeting with others around the globe.

There are quite a few challenges around this, mainly because participants at the actual meeting sometimes forget to speak into the microphone (which is shared) and so a lot of conversation is lost. It's also unfortunately the case that often that a couple of people have a whispered conversation while the main discussion is ongoing. This has a negative impact on the remote participants as they can hear some noise in the background and can't follow the overall discussion.

In its 2015 Industry Forecast, Advito didn't see any uptake in these hybrid events, though this doesn't mean they're not happening. Rather, they're internal meetings that companies might not even consider a 'meeting' in the sense of business travel. What Advito did see is a new demand for fully virtual meetings.

Virtual Meetings

Lastly, let's look at virtual meetings as they're part of this industry as well and, together with virtual collaboration, might have a bigger impact on corporate travel overall. When virtual started it was thought to have a dramatic impact on business travel. Advocates said that the need for meeting in person would be eliminated through technology and virtual 'face-to-face' options.

So far, it hasn't come to that. Although virtual meetings are being used, they're supplementing travel rather than substituting it – at least for the moment.

Virtual Meetings: A Definition

While virtual meetings can be as 'simple' as telephone conferences, they can also be as complex as a live video chat across multiple locations, or an online-only conference with avatars.

The non-profit association EDUCAUSE® (2006) committed to advancing higher education, gives this definition:

> *'Virtual meetings are real-time interactions that take place over the internet using integrated audio and video, chat tools and application sharing.'*

This is a good overall definition, but let's take a look at some forms of virtual meetings that are popular and emerging:

Telephone Conference Call	Participants dial into a special code and are connected with others across the globe. This is audio only.
Webinar / Webex	Participants access a website (usually they have to sign up for this service) and listen in on a seminar or panel discussion, while following a presentation on screen. A chat feature is normally enabled to ask questions.
Video Conference Call	Same as the telephone conference call, though with the addition of video transmission. This means participants can actually see each other (usually via webcams).
Online-only conference	Participants receive log-in details and are prompted to create an avatar (a virtual personality representing them in the conference); the avatar walks through the conference (quite like a computer game) and can talk to other participants using a chat feature. Presentations and key notes can be accessed through video links and are available at a later date as well.

Virtual Meetings and Corporate Travel

Chief Financial Officers (CFOs) are very interested in virtual meetings on the premise that they reduce travel costs. However, as mentioned before, so far, virtual meetings have run alongside travel – rather than substituting it.

In March 2015 BTN published a story about how Sony Mobile Communications is trying to persuade employees to use more virtual technologies (Cohen, 2015). To do this, it's invested heavily in supporting infrastructure, opening smaller telepresence units across multiple office locations.

To ensure uninterrupted access of both the telepresence service as well as daily internet use, the virtual meeting infrastructure is installed on separate servers.

So far, the story continues, Sony Mobile hasn't seen the envisioned impact, but the travel manager believes this is only a matter of time and education. Since Sony Mobile doesn't mandate travel, they rely on communications and good technology as advocates for virtual meetings.

Virtual Meetings Trends

The two biggest trends are holographic imaging and crowd-sourcing. They're on very opposite ends with the one being made for the few and the other enjoyed by the many.

Holographic Meetings

Last year nh Hotels introduced hotel catering specifically for the business traveller. Next to offering amenities without surcharge, such as ironing, dry-cleaning, shoe-shining and in-room dining services, they launched virtual meetings made possible in every hotel room.

And it didn't end there: they also offered holographic meetings! (Meetpie 2014) There are two options (both at additional cost it might be said):

- ◆ Recording a message that can be played back with a hologram display of the speaker.

- ◆ Using live holographic conferencing (this option is rather expensive due to the vast amount of data that is transmitted).

It was showcased and introduced at the Global Business Travel Association's (GBTA) annual European conference in Berlin in 2014. Participants of the show had a chance to see and 'interact' with the hologram (though this was a recording). It was received well by the crowds, though no one wanted to say whether this was going to be something that would offer true value.

Crowd-sourcing

While not your typical virtual meeting, crowd-sourcing is here and is going to grow. Essentially, it lets a vast number of people share ideas, interests and knowledge, to vote for them and even make something tangible from them.

They're virtual meetings where participants voluntarily (and by personal desire) step in and, often, help out with money or other resources, like time.

So how does crowd-sourcing impact tourism in general and business travel in particular? At the moment it's happening around travel advice and tips of where to stay or eat when abroad (Higgins 2011). But will it have an actual impact on business travel? Honestly, I don't know – yet. But if an idea about how to make business travel easier gets heard and backed by a crowd, it's going to be the next big thing for sure.

Summary

Chapter one sets the scene, looking at the overall importance of tourism for the global economy and subsequently looking at corporate travel, MICE and even virtual meetings in turn.

Business travel is the umbrella term for any business–related travel; hence the individual's travel is part of it. In this book, we use the term corporate travel to distinguish this form of travel from the others, bearing in mind that the word 'corporate' is loosely used to represent any profession (and so could be government, NGO or university as well).

Corporate travel needs to be managed and the later chapters offer a detailed picture of what this means. And with total business spend in the US alone at $280.2 billion in 2014 it's easy to imagine why corporate travel management is needed.

Yet that doesn't mean that other parts of business travel aren't important. MICE, meetings and events, or plainly the meetings industry, plays an important part in driving economic success. Remember, there are two sides of the coin, and this book looks at the individual traveller's needs and support systems – rather than those of the meeting's organiser.

The meetings industry, similarly to corporate travel, was hit by the economic downturn of 2008; yet finally in 2014 recovery started to show in this sector. Demand has been more stable, or rising, since, though many budgets are still tightly controlled.

The last part of the chapter about virtual meetings shows how technology is changing the traditional landscape in business travel. And even though virtual is a great way to keep up to speed on projects without always having to travel, they haven't yet had as big an impact as expected. Watch this space!

Now that the scene is set, let's go back to the corporate travel industry and see how it developed over time to what it is today – and just how the future might be going to look like.

Bibliography

Tribe, John. 2011. *The Economics of Recreation, Leisure and Tourism*. 4. Oxford, Great Britain: Butterworth-Heinemann.

UNWTO. 2014. *Glossary of tourism terms*. Accessed July 22, 2015. s3-eu-west-1.amazonaws.com/staticunwto/Statistics/Glossary+of+terms.pdf.

UNWTO. 2015. *UNWTO Tourism Highlights*. United Nations World Tourism Organisation.

—. 2015. *Why Tourism Matters*. Accessed July 27, 2015. www2.unwto.org/content/why-tourism .

whatuni.com. 2015. *Travel and Tourism Degrees*. Accessed July 22, 2015. www.whatuni.com/degrees/courses/degree-courses/travel-and-tourism-degree-courses-united-kingdom/m/united+kingdom/r/5979/page.html.

WTTC. 2015. *Travel and Tourism Economic Impact 2014 World*. World Travel & Tourism Council. Accessed 2015. www.wttc.org/-/media/files/reports/economic%20impact%20research/regional%20reports/world2014.pdf.

WTTC. 2015. *World Travel & Tourism Council League Tables*. World Travel & Tourism Council. Accessed July 22, 2015.

CHAPTER 2
Past, Present and Future

By the end of this chapter you'll be able to:

✓ Explain the beginnings of corporate travel and how these relate to today's tourism industry.

✓ Know key dates, people and developments in the corporate travel industry.

✓ Develop an understanding of the current situation of the industry, including challenges it's facing.

✓ Have insights into trends that are going to have an impact on the industry; and generally an overview of corporate travel's future.

Quick Facts

- Corporate travel, in form of international trade, can be traced back to Egypt – roughly 3,500 years ago.

- Security has played a big part in travel, the Tang dynasty making the Silk Road a safe network for all who travelled as early as 650 AD.

- Today, corporate travel is characterised by its complexities around schedules and choices.

- Trending topics of the year 2016 are the sharing economy, traveller engagement, personalisation, distribution channels, virtual payments, virtual collaboration and predictive and prescriptive analytics.

- Fast forward to 2020 and this will become even more data- and technology-driven with the IoT (Internet of Things) and smart everythings (glasses, cars, cities – you name it).

Introduction

This second chapter focuses on the corporate travel industry: its past, present and future – and how this relates to what we readily consume as tourism today.

You might be aware that it was sales people who started the 'travel hype' back in the day. They travelled to find other people who might want to buy their wares; actually, they wanted to trade their goods as money back then was a thing of the future.

But before we dive into ancient times, let's have a look at how this chapter helps your understanding of the corporate travel industry.

The beginnings go very far back in time, and there are a few key things you should know. Starting with the New Kingdom of Egypt and other ancient empires, ending with the Silk Road (a trading network more than a route), it connected China with Europe. Moving on to Marco Polo, famed by the travelling companion guide books more than by his actual history: his father and uncle made one of the first trips from Italy to China, selling jewellery. What's important to note here is that a business trip back in the day could take more than 10 years, rather than two days.

The time after Marco Polo was driven by trade with the Orient (especially spices) and the Europeans amassed their wealth. But this also meant conflict of interests, finding the best trade routes and pressing competitive advantage. When Christopher Columbus sailed under a Spanish flag to find the New World, he actually set out for a new route to the Orient – with the aim of reducing travel time.

The focus then shifts to the Industrial Revolution – and the big expositions (like the World Fair of 1889 that brought Paris the Eiffel Tower). This leads onto the last 100 years of corporate travel. Industrial and technological advancements during this time make it absolutely worthwhile spending some time here.

With the breakthrough developments of 3,500 years in mind, next is the current situation – today's corporate travel. Reading a little about corporate travel management in the first chapter, this is going to let you in on what's happening in the market place. What has the industry been up to lately? What are the current challenges? Which issues have been solved recently? And possibly most importantly: where is the industry heading next?

Similarly to the meetings industry, corporate travel is still facing tight budgets. This is possibly due to more trips being taken, but less money being spent while on the road. To better understand and communicate with travellers, many companies are now turning to traveller engagement: a way to open dialogue with travellers, explaining to them what's happening in the travel programme and why, and generating ownership of travel policy.

This leads on to a discussion of hypes and trends, differentiating these two and forecasting which might have an impact and which will fade, which will develop into something different and which will be the next big thing.

Data analytics are big everywhere, especially with the hype created by the media around Big Data. But what is that exactly and why does the corporate travel industry need to know? It's just one of the trends that's going to be discussed so stay tuned.

The chapter is rounded off with a more general outlook on corporate travel in the future.

The Past: 1500 BC to 1900 AD

There is little information available on corporate travel, at least in written (and somewhat academic) format. As stated in chapter one, there's been very limited academic interest, so far, in this form of tourism: partly because of accessibility to the industry; partly because it's not been recognised as an industry in its own right.

However, John Swarbrooke and Susan Horner wrote a book titled 'Business Travel and Tourism' in 2001, which offers a comprehensive overview of the beginnings of corporate travel.

To get an at-a-glance understanding, have a look at this graphic:

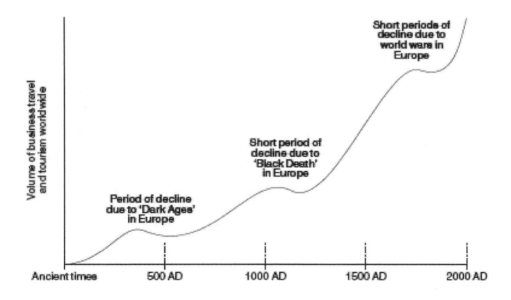

Figure 1 – Growth of Business Travel and Tourism

It's reprinted from the above mentioned book, and, as the authors freely admit, it's not based on actual data, but drawn up as 'a comprehensive, if highly generalized, view of the historical growth of business travel and tourism' (Swarbrooke & Horner, 2001).

However, records show that trade started much earlier than the graphic depicts; around 1500 BC Egyptians were already trading up and down the Nile.

Travel to Trade

Trading commenced when people settled and became versed in agriculture (growing crops and herding animals). When they found they had more than they needed for personal consumption, they started looking for options to trade goods. In the beginning this might have been within one settlement where grain was swapped for wool, but in the ancient empires trade started to flourish beyond village borders.

The New Kingdom of Egypt

Based on the country's vast resources, Egypt developed much faster than its counterparts in the North. The New Kingdom of Egypt saw a rich culture emerging between 1550–1070 BC – about 500 years of relative political stability and wealth (Roerig, 2015). Helped by the Nile to transport goods, and by the discovery of gold mines, the kingdom flourished led by the pharaohs and dependent on the labour its people.

Hatshepsut is the first female pharaoh who co-reigned with Thutmose III (her infant nephew) between ca. 1476–1458 BC (Tyldesley, 2015). Her reign was dominated by trade, especially sea trade with Punt, *'a trading centre (since vanished) on the East African coast beyond the southernmost end of the Red Sea'. This is likely to be the earliest record of 'business travel' on a regional scale.*

Travel to Share Knowledge

Another important reason to travel is sharing knowledge and information. In ancient times this was particularly important as administrative systems like the ones we're used to today through our governments were just starting to develop.

Because sharing knowledge is so important, language and culture play a large part in its development. And so does a currency system to base value for goods and services. Both had their beginnings in the Persian Empire.

The Persian Empire

Quite some 500 years after the New Kingdom of Egypt fell into demise, the Persian empire began to blossom. Seeing that the Persian empire can still be traced into modern day Iran, the different eras are referred to by the family name that established it. In this case, the Achaemenid Empire, which was the largest the ancient world had seen, lasted from around 550 to 330 BC (Ancient History Encyclopedia, 2011).

After the expansion of the empire under Cyrus the Great, his son Darius I is most known for his humanitarian approach to rulership. The ancient city of Persepolis is based on his self-image as a king. Under his many achievements, the ones that concern us most are the 'Royal Road' – a stretch of 2,500 kilometres – and his establishment of silver and gold coins for trading (Iran Chamber Society, n.d.).

The exchange of commodities throughout the empire was, at the height of Darius's reign, so great and absolute that words from the Persian marketplaces still have a place in today's vocabulary, examples are, *"bazaar, shawl, sash, turquoise, tiara, orange, lemon, melon, peach, spinach and asparagus"* (Iran Chamber Society, n.d.). And this shows just how important travel is for the development and understanding of cultures as well as the long-lasting effect it can have.

Travel to Innovate

When travel was more or less the norm to participate in the trading of commodities and information, the desire for merging old with new, known with unknown, became more prevalent.

If ever you chance a look at the map of the Roman Empire (in its heyday) you'll see they enclosed the whole of the Mediterranean Sea (plus England and Wales); they had to communicate with very different cultures and find ways to engage.

The Roman Empire

Note that even though Rome (the Kingdom) was already founded in 753 BC, it wasn't until 27 BC that the Roman Empire became the superpower in the Mediterranean region. Its supremacy lasted until 476 AD (BBC, 2014).

The Romans built a vast infrastructure, including not only highways but also waterways and aqueducts. They were great city planners and had a code of law joining Greek and Roman philosophies and traditions. They learnt from others and incorporated alien traditions into their own. This was innovation at its best and, naturally, trade and commerce flourished.

But the Romans may also be remembered for their favour of luxuries and the invention of the Roman Baths. In Europe today there are many cities named after these spas (e.g. Baden Baden, Germany and Bath, United Kingdom). One could argue that thus the Romans were the first to mix business with pleasure; they would go to a spa to relax after travelling.

Note that the word 'spa' is actually the name of a city in Belgium. There was an iron-bearing spring that was often called upon to cure those with iron deficiency.

In the 21st century, SPA was said to be an acronym for sanitas per aquam (health through water), but this is a modern-day creation!

Travel to Explore and Educate

Finally, we're moving towards the explorers: People who travelled to learn about the world, find out new things and then educate those who didn't travel back home.

But before moving on to the big names, like Polo, Columbus and, later, James Cook, let's have a look at the first truly international trade network:

The Silk Road

The Silk Road is possibly a phrase many people have associations with. Some will immediately connect it with the trading network that span from China to Europe as early as 500 BC (Silkroad Foundation, 2000). Others will think of the somewhat recent drug scandal and what's called the dark web – but you'll need to get another book to find out more about that.

It's important to understand, even though we use the term Silk Road (or Silk Route), it actually was a network of roads, connecting what's now Xi'an (think Terracotta Warriors) with Istanbul (think Hagia Sophia) via many different points.

Silk fabric can be traced back in Europe to around 500 BC, however, trading became more frequent under the Han Dynasty (202 BC-9 AD). Naturally, many more commodities were traded on this route, and the name has only been coined in the 19th century.

This international road network saw its peak during the Tang Dynasty (618–906 AD). Under the rule of Emperor Taizong, the overland trade routes were kept safe as he secured peace with the nomadic tribes from the north and northwest (Travel China Guide, 2015).

Yet even without fear of warring tribes, the terrain isn't easy. The route travels through the Taklimakan desert, stretching from Urumqi in the north to the Himalayas in the south and crossing various mountain ranges (Silkroad Foundation, 2000). Travel was usually done only on a stretch of the road so merchants would pass their wares on to others who would take them a bit further and exchange again.

Marco Polo

As mentioned in the introduction to this chapter, it was actually Marco's father and uncle who were the first European travellers to come all the way to China (at least known to us). Note that before them, Giovanni di Piano Carpini in 1245 and Guillaume de Rubrouck in 1253 made the journey all the way to the Mongolian capital Karakorom by the request of Pope Innocent IV (Campbell, 2016).

The acclaimed and well-documented journey of Marco Polo lasted three-and-a-half years (1271-1275), travelling from Venice to Beijing.

Much of our understanding of Mongolian and Chinese culture in the 13th century is based on these travel accounts of Marco Polo. It goes to show that travel, exploration and education go hand in hand – and can have a very long-lasting influence.

Christopher Columbus

Another well-known name: the discoverer of America. Or India – as he thought. And not even the true discoverer (this happened about 500 years earlier through the Vikings). Yet, at that point in time, it was very important for Europeans to realise there was land that still needed exploring! And while Polo travelled the land, Columbus travelled the sea – about 200 years later.

To understand the importance of Columbus' mission we need to appreciate the race for resources, trade and wealth happening throughout Europe at the time. Columbus was convinced that he could offer his sponsoring nation a distinct competitive advantage by cutting down travel times, going by sea, rather than by road. He approached the Portuguese, French and English courts before finding backing for his trip in Spain (Encyclopaedia Britannica, 2015).

The journey from Palos de la Frontera, Spain, to the Bahamas in 1492 took 10 weeks and is largely accepted as the first Atlantic exploration.

Full Circle: Travel to do it All

Before taking a look at global corporations, like the East India Tea Company, let's quickly remind ourselves that this historic overview is by no means conclusive. Many dates, people and events have been left out because to name them all would fill more than one book alone.

There is, however, one more name, the European father of trade, finance systems and charity: Francesco Datini (1335–1410). On the 'small scale' of Europe he operated the first managed travel to 'do it all': trade, share knowledge, innovate and educate (Encyclopaedia Britannica, 2015). And all of this before Columbus ever sat sail!

But now let's move on to the next 400 years of history, and please remember that the political atrocities happening during this time aren't part of this summary – but that doesn't by any means mean they are forgotten!

The East India Tea Company

On New Year's Eve in 1600, Queen Elizabeth I granted the Royal Charter to the East India Tea Company. Little did she know that this would be the cornerstone of Britain's supremacy for (roughly) the next 250 years.

The East India Tea Company is possibly the first to create branding for their corporation. What started out as a simple stamp developed into the first logo (Boston Tea Party, 2016) and stood for the origin of the wares, as well as their quality (EastIndiaCompany, 2014).

The corporation was built to travel for trade; sharing knowledge was an important by-product to find out about markets and opportunities (and keeping well ahead of the competition, like the Dutch East India Company). Innovation is most apparent in the systematic approach to doing and accounting for business; and even thought the world had already been discovered by their time, there was a lot to explore yet.

Figure 2 The East India Tea Company

Captain James Cook

Though he wasn't directly linked to the East India Tea Company, his journeys happened during their 'rule' over the trade to Asia. The explorer has quite a long list of achievements to his name, including the cartography of Australia, New Zealand, Polynesia and Micronesia. Having learned surveying and charting in the Royal Navy, Europe had to change its perceptions of the world thanks to him (Wikipedia, 2014).

His first voyage started in 1768 from Plymouth, UK, and landed in Gisborne, New Zealand, after just one year; stopping en route in Tahiti to observe the transit of Venus across the sun (BBC, 2014).

Figure 3 – Expo at Crystal Palace, London, 1851

The World Exhibitions

World exhibitions started in the later part of the 18th century but became more important with the Great Exhibition of 1851 at the Crystal Palace (built for the occasion) in Hyde Park, London. On display were technological advancements so visitors could see the whole production process of cotton, art, machinery and jewels as well as colonial raw materials.

A world exhibition 'reverse engineers' travel in as much as you didn't have to travel around the world to visit the exhibition; the exhibition came to your country: exhibits are put on show from many countries around the globe and people travel to the exhibition to see these artefacts, to explore, be educated and share information. The trade part is the admission fee between one shilling (today £ 4.89) and £1 (£ 3,075).

In London 1851, the Great Exhibition was visited by about six million people between 01 May and 11 October – this was a third of the population at the time. The picture below depicts the Crystal palace built for the occasion (Lienhard 7).

Moving Merchandise: Rail

The invention of the steam-engine locomotive in 1804 and the resulting expansion of the rail network meant that Britain moved from 98 miles of tracks in 1830 to 10,433 miles in 1860 (Bloy, 2013).

In 1842, railway companies commenced passenger services, which were an immediate success: trebling passenger numbers from 1842-1850 and doubling in the 1850s and 1860s again. Yet that wasn't all the economic and social change they brought about: railway transport also meant cheap(er) transportation of goods and easier distribution of perishable goods, thus providing a more varied diet for the nation.

Daily average visitor numbers were around 43,000, with a peak of almost 110,000 visitors on 07 October (Appleton, 1862).

Thomas Cook

You're most probably familiar with the name and the services the company offers today: holidays. But did you know that Thomas Cook was the first to organise group trips and travel arrangements on scale?

In 1841 he took about 500 people on a train from Leicester to Loughborough – 12 miles. But what started small would soon become a national endeavour, with trips to Scotland and to the World Exhibition in London in 1851. Some 150,000 people, including 3,000 children, visited the exhibition by his arrangement (Thomas Cook, n.d.).

The significance of Cook for travel and tourism is undebatable. And he's also important for corporate travel. He's possibly the first to have created a hotel-voucher system: if you bought a voucher for a meal or an overnight stay and the hotel was in his guide book, you could use it for payment.

But now let's move on and take a look at some more recent developments in corporate travel over the last 100 years.

Moving People: Airplanes

The Wright Brothers (Orville and Wilbur) are credited with inventing and building the first successful plane in 1903 (Smithsonian, n.d.).

The Learjet 23 is the first small jet aircraft to enter mass production in 1963: 100 are sold until 1965. It fits seven passengers (including pilots) into a fully pressurised cabin.

The Past: the Last 100 Years

Very timely for this publication, American Express Global Business Travel recently launched a timeline with annual events and achievements for the industry. The following was largely influenced by their research (GBT, 2015), but not all facts have made it into this book.

1920s

The years after WWI focused on business development and technology advances. Ships for passengers and cargo traversed the seas – the fastest being the *Cap Arcona that made the trip from Hamburg, Germany to Buenos Aires, Argentina in just 15 days* (Talbot-Booth, 1936).

But using ships for passenger transport to get to business meetings or do site visits took very long and was soon going to be a thing of the past.

- *QANTAS, THE WORLD'S OLDEST AIRLINE*

  The world's oldest airline still operating today started as a survey flight to drop provisions in the outback (Qantas, n.d.).

- *HERTZ, THE FIRST RENTAL CAR COMPANY*

  In 1923 John Hertz, president of the Yellow Cab Manufacturing Company, bought the Chicago-based car rental concern from William Jacobs, who had started the business five years earlier, and had already generated annual revenues of $1 million (Hertz, 2015).

- *SHIPPING COMPANIES FUND LUFTHANSA*

  NDL (North German Lloyd) and HAPAG (Hamburg-Amerikanische-Packetfahrt-Actien-Gesellschaft) built their first successful merger by venturing from shipping into civil aviation. In 1926 they became Deutsche Lufthansa and flew more than 6,000km on liner services across Europe daily (Hapag-Lloyd, n.d.).

1930s

A decade which saw women enter not only business travel, but also play a more prominent role in business in general.

- *BOEING: THE FIRST STEWARDESS*

  Ellen Church, a trained nurse and pilot, convinced Boeing that nurses should accompany flights because of the general fear of flying of the public (Wikipedia, 2015).

- *THE FIRST COMPANY WWNED AND MANAGED BY A WOMAN*

  This was established by Tillie Lewis who travelled to Italy to learn about traditional tomato growing. Back in California she started her own company, Flotill Products Inc., canning Italian-inspired tomatoes (Online Archive of California, n.d.).

- *BUSINESSWOMEN AT HOTEL ASTOR*

  One of the first gatherings of businesswomen, aspiring businesswomen and corporations with the Institute of Women's Professional Relations in 1935 (GBT, 2015).

1940s

The 40s see the worst of WWII, but also its end. The business ideas, dormant for 10 years, are thriving and falling on fruitful soil.

- *NEW YORK'S FIRST FASHION SHOW: PRESS WEEK*

  In 1943, Eleanor Lambert invited fashion journalists to New York for a press week. She jumped at the chance to bring American fashion into the media, as journalists couldn't travel to Paris (Fortini, 2015).

- *CREATION OF THE INTERNATIONAL MONETARY FUND (IMF)*

  A meeting of representatives of 45 countries in 1944 agreed the establishment of the IMF as soon as the war was over; their main aim was to avoid a repetition of the Great Depression of the 1930s (IMF, n.d.).

- *THE VISION FOR DISNEYLAND*

  It was at the Chicago Railroad Fair of 1948 that it is said Walt Disney solidified his idea of a Disney-inspired amusement park — which he then established back at home in California. What he liked most was the opportunity to interact with the exhibits and look 'behind the scenes' (Wikipedia, 2015).

1950s

Suppliers start looking into business travel: challenges of bookings, as well as getting about and staying overnight.

- *AMERICAN AIRLINES + IBM = SABRE*

  When American Airlines President C.R. Smith met IBM Senior Sales Representative R. Blair Smith on a chance encounter on a flight from Los Angeles to New York, they set the ground work for the first real-time reservation system (Sabre, n.d.).

- *TOYOTA: EXPORTING SMALL PASSENGER CARS TO THE US*

  In 1957 Toyota saw a market niche in the US: small passenger cars. They established an international head quarter in the same year. They became the first import manufacturer to sell over 1 million vehicles (Toyota, 2015).

◆ **Hilton Hotels: opening a string of airport hotels**

Noticing the business travel trend and resulting needs, Hilton opened a string of 300-unit hotels at airport locations as early as 1958 (GBT, 2015).

1960s

The world's getting bigger and better: consumption is almost an 'art nouveau', emerging after the hardship years.

◆ **New York World Fair**

Over 110 years after the Great Exhibition at London's Crystal Palace, New York held a World Fair in 1964 themed 'Peace through Understanding'. More than 51 million attended this last display of a grand consumer show (Wikipedia, 2016).

◆ **Hilton Lady**

Seeing an increase in women travellers, Hilton hotels launch Hilton Lady in 1965. Selected hotels offer women-only floors, and special amenities in rooms (Hilton Worldwide, 2015).

◆ **First flight of Boeing's 747**

In 1969, Boeing conducts the first 747 flight – the most successful airplane to date. The jumbo jet can carry up to 450 passengers and has a range of about 6,000 miles (Stein, 2001).

1970s

Technology advances and with these come exciting new times in the travel industry – and beyond its borders.

◆ **Federal Express is born**

In 1971, Frederick Smith buys controlling stakes in Arkansas Aviation Sales to test a theory he'd written a term paper about at Yale University: passenger routes aren't economically viable for cargo. In 1973, the company Federal Express launched with 14 planes and 186 packages for 25 clients (FedEx, 2016).

◆ **The beginnings of Microsoft**

Paul Allen and Bill Gates formed their partnership to write a BASIC code for the MITS Altair computer. This was the beginning, not only of Microsoft, but also of modern-day personal computing (Microsoft, 2015).

◆ **Concorde takes flight**

1976 sees Concorde introduced into commercial service. It halves the flying time from London to New York to 3.5 hours and can carry up to 100 passengers. Sadly, it had to cease operations after a fatal accident in July 2000 (National Academy of Engineering, 2015).

1980s

The 80s start focusing on the actual traveller – and consumer. Drawing out differences in client groups, segmentation is starting.

◆ *LAUNCH OF THE FIRST BUSINESS CLASS*

While first class was 'standard' on all airlines, Pan American became the first carrier to introduce a business class for the increasing numbers of corporate travellers. This service was known as clipper class (Cusack, n.d.).

◆ *CHANGING COFFEE CULTURE IN AMERICA*

In 1983, a trip to Italy convinced Starbuck's marketing manager Howard Schultz to introduce Italian-style coffee bars in the US. Serving espressos was not only the first step away from selling high-quality coffee beans – but also a step towards becoming a global phenomenon (Tuck School of Business at Dartmouth, 2011).

◆ *PIMP MY SUITCASE*

A 747 airline pilot from Northwest Airlines invented the first suitcase on wheels, called Rollaboard. This was the beginning of Travelpro International and changed the way luggage could be less of a burden – even on long-haul trips (Travelpro, 2016).

1990s

Travel really started to be for the masses – in leisure and corporate alike. There was also a distinct shift in corporate travel towards finding more efficient ways of doing business – on a global scale.

◆ *THE WORLD WIDE WEB*

Hard to believe, but the world wide web, http addresses and URLs were made available through the internet in 1993. The objective of the project then was to connect computers without having to be in the same physical location (Webfoundation, 2015). And good thing, too, that corporate travel still flourishes.

◆ *GLOBALISATION: WINE IMPORTS*

At a wine show in California, New Yorker Bill Deutsch and Australian John Casella met; the former to buy wine, the latter to sell. This 50/50 joint venture started in 1999, but only took off in 2001 after rebranding to the now household name 'YellowTail' (GBT, 2015).

◆ *GLOBALISATION: CALL CENTRES*

In 1998 the first Indian call centre opened with 18 employees to answer US customer service calls. The man behind the idea: Pramod Bhasin. Today, this industry is employing hundreds of thousands across the subcontinent (BBC, 2015).

2000s

The new millennium started with a shock for the travel industry: the attacks on the World Trade Center in New York are engraved on everyone's memory. And they have had an impact. But that wasn't the only thing happening – and there are some good stories, too.

- ◆ *SECURITY AND TRAVEL RISK MANAGEMENT*

  9/11 has been the most prominent attack for the travel industry (though sadly not the only one). Subsequently, access to the cockpit was forbidden and a complex security door installed. On the ground, security controls were tightened and still today we have to grapple with tiny bottles of toiletries when travelling without hold luggage (Logan, 2008).

- ◆ *VIRTUAL COLLABORATION: SKYPE*

  The popular voice over internet protocol (VOIP) provider launched in 2003. Video and chat functions complemented this tool, which is now part of the Microsoft empire (Wikipedia, 2016). Another step towards the reduction in necessary travel was taken – though again, it didn't come with the savings hoped for.

- ◆ *ON-DEMAND ECONOMY*

  2008 saw the launch of UberCab in San Francisco. It lets customers call chauffeur-driven cars through the simple push of a button on a mobile app. What started small is now operating in 58 countries across the globe – and valued at over $50 billion (McAlone, 2015).

There are many other things that have been going on and are ongoing. This list doesn't claim to be definitive, but it provides a viewpoint of a changing world – and how corporate travel fits in.

Present: Where Are We Now?

With about 3,500 years of historical background in mind, it's now time to look at the present. Where is corporate travel now? What's currently being discussed in the industry? What are the backbone topics; those that will always play a part? And what are the hype topics people flock towards? Let's deepen your understanding of this part of corporate travel.

Corporate Travel Today

In a way there are very few changes to travel compared to back in the Roman Empire – yet, looking at it from the other side, a Roman traveller would hardly know his way around.

So what's the same? The reasons for travel haven't changed: it's still mainly for business (or trade), sharing information (internally or externally), innovating (in-company or in collaboration with others) and exploring/educating (new business ventures and social media).

Faster Travel Times and More Options

What has changed is the means of travel. Remember all the stories of the explorers you've just read? Well, here's a little something for you to put that in perspective. Today's travel times are taken from Skyscanner (Skyscanner, 2015).

Who & When	From & To	Travel Time	Travel Now
Marco Polo, 1271	Venice to Beijing	3.5 years	13 hours
Christopher Columbus, 1492	Seville to Nassau	10 weeks	18 hours
James Cook, 1768	Plymouth to Gisborne	1 year (with stopover)	30 hours

Travel has got a lot faster – and also much more convenient. We often forget the conditions travellers had to endure only 100 years ago.

But it's not only travel that has got faster (and everything else in life, it seems), there's a lot more options to choose from today as well. The aforementioned Skyscanner is a web service providing a search engine for flights. You just plug in where you want to start, where you want to go and the dates you'd like to travel. And then, after a couple of seconds buffering time, you have pages and pages of results – multiple airlines, direct connections or those where you change planes through a hub to make the journey cheaper, but also longer.

There are many services like Skyscanner; meta-search engines for air and hotel alike. And many people use them to find the best options for their trip, filtered by convenient times, total travel time or (most often) price. And it's services like this that hamper the efforts of the travel manager.

Corporate Travel Complexities

More suppliers, more choices and less time spent on the road means there's also a lot more complexity. Questions arise as to which supplier is the best fit? Should the traveller get there quickly, cheaply or comfortably? Or all at the same time?

Then there are other things to consider which we will look at in more detail throughout this book: duty of care, negotiations, company goals, budgets, national and international travel, payments, safety and standards, data – the list is almost endless.

When the (business) world got more complex, companies looked for ways to ensure optimised processes for travel. They came to realise that they needed an intermediary and the concept for the travel management company (TMC) was born. The job of the TMC was mainly to book and make travel arrangements – but this has changed over the years. Today, TMCs are called upon to provide much more than tickets and itineraries. They have to be 'partners', 'trusted advisors', and help their client companies achieve goals of saving costs – while still making a profit themselves. We look at TMCs and their role in a bit more detail in chapter three.

What's important to know for this chapter is that corporate travel is complex. It's not 'just booking a flight' – there's implications and a lot of stakeholders. Corporate travel isn't a B2C (business to consumer) relationship: it's a B2B(2B)2C relationship. And that's just adding to the confusion.

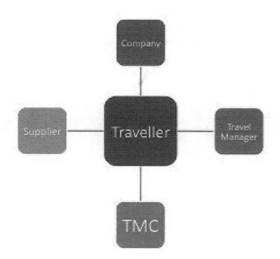

It's essential to understand who does what for whom. The following table aims to make this a bit easier to understand.

Company	Hires a travel manager (or outsources the position) to supervise company travel in alignment with its company goals.
Travel Manager	Hires a TMC to help with supplier negotiations and overall travel arrangements.
Traveller	Calls the TMC (or uses the online booking tool) to arrange travel.
TMC	Makes the booking and advises the travel manager about all questions regarding corporate travel.
Supplier	Fulfils travel arrangements.
Traveller	Travels and makes use of the services.

Yet it's not just a linear process. One of my favourite books, *Predictably Irrational* by Dan Ariely (2009), is about how people aren't perfect nor are they rational. Purchase decisions might be well thought through, but they depend on the information one reads and accesses at the time and on the people in your personal network with whom you might discuss your options.

Corporate travel isn't different, and, even though travel managers would like to see perfect, rational employees (who, after all, signed a contract to work with the company so should play by the rules), they are faced with mere mortals; people who might be swayed by loyalty programmes and perks.

Though it isn't fair to blame just the travellers for bending the rules here and there, everyone in the chain contributes – consciously and subconsciously – to the complexities:

- ◆ The company hires the travel manager who appears to be the best candidate for the job – that doesn't necessarily have to be the case (though it definitely could be). There's an element of personal fit for the company, and, quite frankly, sympathy.

- ◆ The travel manager runs a request for proposal (RFP) to compare different TMCs and their services and select the right one for the company. Here, again, there's an element of sympathy and, quite possibly, history: if the travel manager has had a similar role before, or worked in the industry, they might well have developed a liking for a particular provider.

- ◆ The TMC books the travel arrangements for the traveller in accordance with the preferred supplier programme of the company. However, within that programme there might be a supplier that has a preferred relationship with the TMC and is therefore pushed by the agent (to earn a higher commission or reach a goal to win an incentive).

◆ The supplier fulfils the travel and you might think that they're blame-free. But have a quick look at the apps on your phone: any loyalty programmes on there? Frequent fliers? Hotel stays? Yes, I thought so! Suppliers are the ones getting the travellers into trouble in the first place by crafting a personal relationship with them and giving extra — for travellers who come back often (and book) direct.

Also don't forget the TMCs and suppliers need to MAKE money, while the companies and travel managers need to SAVE money. And the travellers? They want a hassle-free, comfortable travel experience.

Regional Differences in Corporate Travel

Now that you're a little more familiar with the process and the complexity of corporate travel, let's have a look at some regional differences as well. But before, let's be honest, these are generalisations (just like the examples above) and will not make sense in all situations or for all companies — so, as usual, take the following with a pinch of salt.

When looking at regions in corporate travel it's generally about demand and supply for air and hotel (and sometimes car rental and meetings). For example, Advito publishes an annual forecast (and quarterly updates) looking at these categories. CWT has partnered with GBTA to provide a forecast on an annual basis. Both look at fare and rate increases (or decreases), economic situation and the oil price. And there's some debate about how many regions there are: GBTA's forecast looks at four regions (GBTA, 2015), while Advito's looks at seven (Advito, 2015).

CWT/GBTA	Advito
North America	North America
Latin America	Latin America
EMEA	Europe
	Middle East
	Africa
Asia	Asia
	Southwest Pacific

This is generally based on data availability for the regions. And from a 'valuable information' perspective it makes sense to separate Europe from Middle East and Africa (such a vast continent) and also to separate Australia and New Zealand (building Southwest Pacific) from the rest of Asia – which, again, is very big on its own and very different.

So what are the differences? North America can generally be labelled as the 'early adopters': topics that hype today in North America will hype in Europe about six to 12 months later (this is not scientifically proven, but rather drawn from my experience working in the field). And it's not only the hype, they also follow through much quicker with new product adoption.

Europe is generally lagging behind North America, partly because of more stringent data protection laws and partly because of language issues. A good example is the introduction of gamification (employing game-like components to the planning and booking stages of travel in order to increase compliance) to the market in 2011. It was brought to market by Coca-Cola first in the US. (Mcnulty, 2011), but it took close to 18 months to set up something similar in Germany (Campbell J. , 2013).

Latin America and Asia are relatively new regions for corporate travel management. This follows from companies' global expansions and increased need to fly out to their local subsidiaries. Development of corporate travel in these regions started often with implementing a proven travel manager from North America or Europe in the offshore offices. But now there are many more locals involved in running corporate travel, which is bringing new ideas to the industry.

Both regions profit from the legacy of traditionally built-up travel management, but have the necessary resources to jump ahead of the queue and make best use of newly developed technologies as well.

Middle East is a region heavily influenced by the Gulf Carriers (Emirates, Qatar Airways and Etihad Airways), which are all trying to pull more business through their hubs. For hotel programmes in this region it's interesting to see loyalty being a much higher priority than savings.

One of the biggest regions, yet largely unexplored for corporate travel, is Africa. Due to conflicts, wars, terrorist activities and epidemics like the Ebola crisis in 2015, the continent is just building up its infrastructure to attract more frequent corporate business (at least for the so-called 'western traveller', as there are many Chinese corporations already investing heavily in the region).

Lastly, Southwest Pacific, that is Australia and New Zealand. They're largely on a par with Europe in terms of the adoption of new products. Yet they're also often doing 'their own thing'; rather than following mainstream trends in corporate travel, they pick and choose what works in their environment.

Travel Management Concerns

So if the traveller really wants a hassle-free, comfortable travel experience, what is so bad about them searching online for the best connection and deal? Shouldn't it be applauded that employees care and try to even save money for the company?

Yes, the general attitude is good! But not completely thought through, as we'll discover when we now explore some of the most common travel-management concerns.

Duty of Care

Imagine you work for a large corporation with +10k employees. Of those, 1,500 are frequent travellers. Now imagine you're the person who has to provide duty of care for all of them; trying to sort through bookings and itineraries that you may have been forwarded (but possibly not).

Go a step further and think about what would happen in a crisis situation. Unfortunately, there are threats in the world: terrorist activities, like the bombings in Mumbai 2008, or kidnappings in oil-rich but otherwise poor countries like Nigeria. You'd be the person in charge to ensure the safety and security of your travellers – but how can you do that when they're not booking through a central system?

Negotiated Rates

Did you ever realise that rates for flights and hotels (and often car rentals, too) are negotiated for a year or two? When 'your' traveller goes online and searches for the best deals, they're not going through the company's central system.

That means they're missing out on the rates you've negotiated with the suppliers (more on that in chapter four). Sometimes, they might have checked your system and used the price quoted as a benchmark for their own search. No, they're not viciously trying to show you they can do much better than you; they just don't know the differences of rates, terms and conditions they're getting. Communication and education is key here!

Negotiated rates might appear more expensive at a first-glance comparison.

Let's look at a fictitious example:

London Heathrow (LHR) to New York LaGuardia (LGA)

	Traveller	Negotiated
Air fare	$799	$1000
Luggage	$50/suitcase	Included
Cancellation	No refund	Full refund
Changes to booking	Possible for price difference paid, plus charge of $100	Change any time
Lounge access at LHR	Not included	Included

You may argue that this is a too rosy a picture to be true, and you might be right, but it does illustrate the point: there are a lot of additional benefits the traveller knows little of.

And one more important point: You miss out on this booking for your reporting, meaning it's one less seat bought through the negotiated programme. Your negotiation power is dwindling.

Lost Opportunity

Back to the travellers and their attempt to find the best available deal. When you search for a flight, how do you go about it? The average person checks not only multiple websites (airlines direct, metasearch engines, booking platforms) but also through multiple platforms (apps, browser, mobile web, possibly even calling an agent).

Now have a guess how much time this takes? The average trip search takes about three hours (BCD Travel, 2014). That's a lot of time lost for a person who is employed for a job that doesn't include searching for best travel options.

Data Availability

When your traveller books outside your programme, you are hard-pressed to get the data later. Yes, you'll probably have an expense report, but it won't tie in with your other data streams: booking data, transaction data and credit-card data. We'll explore data and business intelligence in chapter four of this book, but for now, you need to know that travel managers need data for various reasons:

- Supplier negotiations
- Performance monitoring
- Budget tracking
- Presentations
- Communications

By circumventing the company's booking channel, employees are upping the grey-zone figures and making it harder for managers to know their actual travel spend. This, in turn, can lead to increased budget controls – making travelling much less fun for everyone else.

Compliance

This ties in with the data availability mentioned before. Compliance is what travel managers expect of their travellers. It means reading the travel policy and, more importantly, abiding by it (for more information on travel policy turn to chapter four).

If the company wants their employee to book through a certain agent or travel management company (TMC), they're expected to do it (rather than searching the web for hours on end to find a better deal).

Compliance is quite good for air bookings at the moment, with rough estimates around 80%. But for hotels it's a different picture; it's around 50% and that's a big concern for travel managers!

Corporate Travel Industry Topics

Knowing a little more about the current state of affairs in corporate travel, it's time to move on to topics that are driving the industry on. First the ones 'not to miss' – they've been around ages and they're here to stay for a while more. These are the topics you most likely encounter in some way, shape or form at the big conferences (and the small ones).

Planning and On-trip services

Probably the most obvious topic: travel managers are always interested to hear what's out there to make planning and on-trip services easily accessible for travellers. One of the reasons being that travellers who like the interface they work with (online booking tool for planning, for example) will very likely stick to it and, therefore, stay compliant. Of interest in this category is trip authorisation. How can companies make sure travellers are taking trips that are necessary?

Other services include door-to-door planning (instead of the usual airport-to-airport options), which include taxi, car or rail trip opportunities, and also come with a nifty CO_2 emissions calculator (if you use RouteRank that is); restaurant programmes like Dinova and, quite simply, text-based messaging to send reminders about travel policy or transport options.

Travel Risk Management (TRM)

This is a very important topic of corporate travel, not only because of the heightened risk of terrorist attacks. Actually, more because we have so much on our minds and our senses are continuously overloaded with information that we are more prone to lose laptops or mobiles containing sensitive information or a printout that wasn't meant to be printed. And unfortunately, there are still companies suffering from optimism bias: it won't happen to them. Sadly, when it is them, they're unprepared and mitigation becomes very limited and costly.

BCD Travel published a paper to alert companies of the importance to have a TRM programme in place. Depending on the corporate's needs, this might be a quick DIY excel spreadsheet (for example when travel is limited to domestic only); or it might need an external specialist like GEOREACH or the Anvil Group. They analyse past travel data and incidents and come up with a plan that jumps into action when something happens.

Demand and Behaviour Management

Demand management is about influencing the number of trips that are taken. Behaviour management is about influencing the decision of which supplier to use when travelling.

Naturally, corporate travel is mainly about the traveller: shaping the perfect individual who'll do everything by the book (i.e. the travel policy). Influencing demand and behaviour helps travel managers achieve this – at least to some extent.

While demand can be influenced through tools like the aforementioned trip authoriser, there are several ways to influence behaviour. Communications play an essential role to engage with the travellers – but more of that later.

Payment and Expense Management

You might wonder why this has to be a particular topic of interest, as paying for travel is straightforward, right? You couldn't be further from the truth. There are so many ways travel is paid for: corporate credit cards, personal credit cards, business travel accounts, purchase cards and even virtual credit cards.

So, at conferences the benefits (or not) of these are discussed with an emphasis of any new developments. For example, virtual cards and automated payments were quite novel in 2015 – at least for corporate travel – and so they got quite a bit of air-time.

Expenses, too, are important: for the traveller to get their money reimbursed; for the travel manager to find out total trip costs and for the company to know where their money is going. But again it's a complex field: there are very few standards in corporate travel today and that means reporting is all over the place.

The vision is a total end-to-end programme in which travellers plan, book, communicate and expense – all through one user experience (though probably powered by different tools). This would allow for total trip costs to be captured (something that's nearly impossible today – or at least only doable through manual labour over a long period of time).

Programme Support and Analytics

And finally, there's programme support and analytics. We've already mentioned it just above: there are few standards in reporting in this industry. Travel itineraries might all have certain key information, but they don't always have the same name (or field code).

Programme support is about showing companies better ways to save in their existing programme, or trying something new (like a mobile app) and providing data on the identified KPIs (key performance indicators).

This field has got a lot of attention in the past couple of years, ever since the term 'big data' went mainstream. While everyone talks about it, there are very few who understand what is meant by it and what implications it would have to actually look at the full 'big data' picture – including sentiment analysis.

Now you know the big topics of corporate travel. There's hardly a conference going by without these on the agenda (in some novel way perchance; or should I say disguise?). So let's now have a look at some hypes and trends that are hot topics at the moment.

Corporate Travel Industry Trends

Please let me remind you that this book is written in January 2016. The conference season is over for the moment, and many media outlets are publishing trends to watch for the year (or even years) ahead.

In other words, it's the perfect time to write about hypes and trends. Let's have a look at the most common ones currently being discussed in the industry.

Sharing Economy

Airbnb and Uber are quite possibly the best-known examples of the sharing economy – at least in corporate travel. And let's be honest, while it started as a true 'sharing' experience (that is people sharing their assets with others for a small fee to cover costs) it has spiralled into a multi-billion-dollar industry in just 12 months.

While suppliers are concerned about their market share, travel managers are concerned about the whereabouts of their travellers – and whether they're safe. Meanwhile, Airbnb has launched a microsite for business travellers listing specially qualified properties (e.g. they have to be fully available to the traveller – no couch-surfing) and offering reporting for travel managers to integrate with expense systems.

And suppliers are acting, too: Hyatt, after announcing they didn't consider Airbnb a threat to hotel business, acquired a stake in Onefinestay, a competitor business in the UK – just five months later (Schaal, 2015).

Uber, whose business really is chauffeur-driven cars rather than sharing car rides, has run into trouble in Europe where their true sharing services (UberPop) have been banned. However, their business model overall is thriving, especially after coining the new term 'on-demand economy', and many business travellers are using their app.

Hertz car-rental company acquired a stake in a car-sharing business, but has just announced that it's going to sell up (Baker, 2015). Leaving the question in the air: can legacy companies truly engage and manage lean companies? It hasn't worked for the airlines: Lufthansa's LCC (low-cost carrier) Germanwings has been rebranded after just one year in existence to Eurowings – but even so they can't hope to compete with the true LCCs like Ryanair and EasyJet.

Traveller Engagement

Traveller engagement is the new way to talk about demand and behaviour management. It's going away from mandating and towards influencing and empowering.

There are various ways to describe this industry hype, but traveller engagement sums it up best. Other names are traveller satisfaction and traveller friction – which focus more on the state of the traveller than bringing them to the table to decide together what works best.

Advito, the independent consultancy (and sister company to BCD Travel) has created a playbook for traveller engagement (Advito, 2015). Essentially, it's helping travel managers communicate with their travellers. It's also explaining why policy is written in a certain way and why it's best to book through the online booking tool or agency. Furthermore, it's about creating an environment for travellers to give feedback and take ownership – of their decisions, but also of the company's travel policy.

Hotel Distribution

This topic is popping up here and there, but hasn't been very consistent over the last 12 months. Basically, hotels are getting smarter about distribution and yield management. They're trying to follow airlines' example and base their daily room rates on demand.

Currently, hotels offer corporate clients negotiated rates which, in theory, are available to the traveller (and more of that later). This new distribution sees hotels offering a certain percentage discount off the best available rate on the day. Hotels argue that this will work out favourably for corporate clients; buyers say that high-demand cities, like New York, will see them pay much higher rates.

So far only a few corporate clients have switched, and some are very happy with the system, especially when combining it with the traditional method; for example, negotiate daily rates with the hotels for your 10 highest frequented cities, but use dynamically priced rates in less frequented locations (Bhatia, 2014).

NDC and Lufthansa

Airlines are also looking at changing their distribution. Traditionally they're booked through the GDS (global distribution system) in which agents can check for flights, connections and prices – as well as compare offers.

A couple of years ago, IATA (International Air Transport Association) started to push for NDC: new distribution capabilities. This would see airlines being able to price according to who is travelling (i.e. if you're a frequent traveller you'll likely get a preferred price) – at least, that's how the media generally portray it.

But NDC can do more and is largely seen as a welcome new way to enhance personalisation and customisation in the airline industry.

How does Lufthansa fit in? Well, they announced about half a year ago that they'd start charging a €16 fee in September 2015 for all bookings made through a GDS; this fee wouldn't apply for any direct bookings. The announcement was met with scepticism and other airlines haven't followed this move – yet. But, Emirates, for example, have countered by making known they're working on their very own distribution system. Whether that will be a plug-in solution for all other airlines to use is to be seen.

The big problem for travel managers (and everyone else who books air travel) is that fares aren't comparable: there's the basic fare, but some include luggage or meals or preferred check-in, etc, which makes it difficult for agents to advise clients and for travellers to get true like-for-like comparisons.

Predictive and Prescriptive Analytics

One of my personal favourites: predictive and prescriptive analytics, though in the industry, they mostly go by 'what-if scenarios'.

Predictive Analytics

Travel managers are very interested in their data, partly to forecast travel spend. Since the economy is seemingly recovering (albeit slowly) they're also more and more interested in making the traveller more comfortable. So how to go about it?

One way is to take past travel data and find out traveller behaviour for booking air travel, for example. The KPIs to look into are:

- Economy ratio (that is, the percentage of how many travellers chose economy rather than business class).
- Advance booking time (that is, how well in advance did travellers book prior to flying out).
- Online booking (that is, how many travellers book through the provided online booking tool).

With this data a model is created and, using historic figures, the travel manager can predict how travellers will behave in future. They can also make changes to the parameters so as to see how it might influence the budget.

In other words, if the travel manager changes the economy class policy, allowing travellers to fly business class for flights over six hours of duration (instead of eight hours), they'll immediately see how that might affect their travel spend.

Prescriptive Analytics

This takes predictive analytics one step further: the travel manager basically just 'tells' the computer how much they want to save, and then gets suggestions like:

- You need to change your economy-class allowance to seven hours flying time to achieve the savings.
- You need to encourage travellers to book on average two days further in advance to achieve the savings.

Naturally it could also be a combination of the KPIs that are looked at.

Data is very important to travel managers because that's how their performance is judged; mainly the savings they achieve. But when they don't have savings, they need to know and show where the money is going – and why it's important that travel spend is maintained at that level.

Virtual Payments

While virtual payments are the norm in everyday personal lives (think PayPal or Apple Wallet), they're just starting to come into corporate travel in the form of virtual credit cards. These are generated by an automated payment tool and provide funds for a certain amount of time and for a specified sum (or spend cap).

They're currently used with some success for hotel bookings and mainly for infrequent travellers (those who don't have access to a corporate credit card or reimbursement processes – like job candidates). However, the market is growing and travellers are pushing to be able to use their mobile wallets for business trips too.

This provides a small overview into the big topics currently under scrutiny in the world of corporate travel. Now let's take it a step further and see what might be talked about in the market next.

Future: Gazing into the Crystal Ball

Let's be honest, if I knew what was going to happen I'd be sitting on the coast somewhere right now rather than writing this book! So while I don't have an actual crystal ball here at the moment, the following are assumptions on my part (and on other's people) of topics that are rumoured to surface soon.

Corporate Travel Tomorrow

Along the lines of the previous chapter, let's take a look at how corporate travel is possibly going to look tomorrow. Remember that these are all topics that are already being discussed – but from media presence it's still quite a long way to make it to mainstream usage. In my opinion they'll come to market within the next five years and will be considered at least somewhat mainstream.

Simpler Data Usage for Decision-Making

Now we all know this to be a paradox: data isn't going to get simpler – rather it's going to be more complex! Yet, the usage of data, especially for the corporate travel industry, is going to change to a more intuitive, simple and interactive way. This, in turn, will lead to better decision-making as trust and confidence in the data increase.

The change is going to be driven primarily through machine learning, whereby a computer learns to look at answers and will be able to highlight problems when they occur. If you're interested in this subject, check out IBM's Watson and the way that's going to improve life in general.

Note though that while this is surely coming, before it really takes off, data-security concerns must be addressed – and overcome. Because even though this will make reporting, analysis, monitoring and predicting so much easier, to be able to do this it will have to access a lot of data which some travellers (and companies) might not be willing to share. There will have to be education and communication around data usage and security to make sure everyone understands what is what, what it's used for and how secure personal data is.

Virtual Payments Continued

We've already looked at how virtual payments are entering corporate travel today. But it's not going to remain a payment option only for the infrequent traveller and their hotel bookings; this is going to take off – and quite soon.

The latest news on the subject came from WEX who announced a new partnership with travel payment platform UATP, providing virtual credit cards to corporate travellers (UATP, 2015). The platform, owned by the world's airlines, is sure to power different payment solutions, including PayPal, Giropay and others that can be used for air, hotel and car-rental bookings.

And virtual cards won't be the only payment option that's going to become mainstream quickly; using a mobile for payments is becoming increasingly more accepted in the consumer world, and, therefore, will be entrenched in corporate travel soon, too. It'll be an interesting development to watch as it closely links back to data security – and how to keep travellers (and their money) safe!

On the flipside, virtual payments will deliver much better data – pinpointed not only to the traveller, but including time of purchase and possibly even a reason for the expenditure. This could all link into an expense tool – and that would mean the traveller fills out his expense report truly on the go; simply by making a payment.

Open Booking

Open booking is a term coined in the last couple of years that means travellers can book through any channel they want, but need to share their booking (or itinerary) with the company so that there's an element of tracking and security. Essentially it's an extension of the 'bring your own device' (BYOD) trend which we've seen across industries lately; use your own, and use the channels you're familiar and happy with.

The hype open booking created quickly died down again as travel managers protested because of duty of care problems (naturally some travellers forgot to forward the itinerary…) and less negotiation power when talking to suppliers. However, technology is making leaps in the way we interact with bookings and purchase behaviour in general.

Open booking is likely to make a return when advances in data capture and standards are in place. This will ensure itineraries are shared with the travel manager and fed back into the database for analysis of travel spend overall, and trip spend specifically. It'll happen as full integration (and digitalisation) becomes more and more the norm.

Safety and Security

There are advances in safety and security, too. Travel risk management, as mentioned earlier, is an important topic – which also ties in with all of the above-mentioned innovations.

So what's going to change? Well, the first wave is going to see more use of trackers: travellers going to higher risk destinations will be 'tracked' to ensure their safety. Means of tracking could be tied to a mobile phone, but there are other wearables that offer the capability.

Geo-fencing is also likely to become more 'normal'; while travellers currently might shudder at the idea of triggering an alarm when leaving a certain area, it's likely there's soon going to be a shift in their thoughts and behaviour – sadly due to all the terrorist activities seen around the world.

A tracking device or geo-fencing allows travel managers (or their hired contractors) to jump into action when an alert is triggered. First contact is established with the traveller to see if help is needed and this could then trigger a rescue mission or evacuation if needed.

Virtual Collaboration and Mobility

Lastly, some thoughts around virtual collaboration and mobility. Virtual is really trying to kick–off in corporate travel. It's actually been trying for a long time, but so far virtual collaboration hasn't really achieved mainstream status.

There are some barriers that have impacted the use of video conferencing in the past: mainly, it used to be seen as a huge investment to implement video facilities in key offices. It's also turned out that those offices that had the technology in place were booked out months in advance – and some people still needed to travel to get to an office with video–conferencing facilities.

But here again technology advances, or rather the scalability that's been achieved over the past years, mean that investments are coming down in size – and so more locations can be transformed to virtual collaboration hubs, reducing the need to travel further.

The last point is mere theory, though, for at the moment there's no proof it's actually bringing the need to travel down. Rather, people see it as a means of communication between face-to-face meetings: video keeps participants better engaged because they have a harder time checking emails or phone messages – which they might be tempted to do during a conference call.

Time is needed to accustom employees to virtual collaboration, and using it between face-to-face meetings is a great first step to start 'trusting' technology. With more advances in file–sharing and virtual white boards (and the like), this shift is definitely going to happen. But don't think people will necessarily travel less!

Corporate Travel: Tomorrow's Trends

Lastly, let's take a look at tomorrow's trends: what will be the new thing that's going to see media attention rise by 2020 and beyond? Let me once again remind you that this is my own opinion and the following is an overview of what I think is going to happen – there's no more foundation to this than experience working and presenting in the corporate travel industry.

Wearable Technology

We can all agree that wearable technologies are already here today – albeit they're just starting out. History tends to repeat itself, although it comes in different disguises. Traditionally, technology trends go mainstream in consumer markets first (that's the B2C markets), before they make their way into the world of corporate travel.

Most recently we've seen it with the developments of mobile apps: after the iPhone 'introduced' smartphones and the market grew globally, companies started designing apps – to make life easier for consumers, but also to build a stronger relationship (dependency) with them. This was around 2010 and it's only now that sophisticated apps for corporate travellers are coming on the market.

So what things might we wear in future? The watch is probably going to be a 'classic' by then. But what about the glasses? Much hyped and then pulled off market, I believe they're going to reappear before too long – and they'll have an impact on all parts of business travel. Imagine, for example, going to a meeting and being able to address everyone by name because the glasses 'recognise' these people?

Hologram Meetings

Think a step further from the glasses, and going back to a point raised in the last chapter, hologram meetings could take off if technology finds a way to interact in real time – when people are actually sitting at their desks or walking to the kitchen for a glass of water.

To me this might be a logical extension of the video conference and virtual collaboration we crave. But it's going to require 'digital natives' to be comfortable in such an environment, and might, therefore, not be something about to happen just yet.

Having said that, with the advances nh hotels have made in holographic messaging, it might not be as far off as we'd (secretly) like to think.

Safety and Security

We've been riding the wave of safety and security quite a bit already in this chapter (and don't think it's going to let up in the pages to come!), but it's a topic that I think we need to keep at the back of our minds. After all, we like to be safe and secure – and hence, should do our best to keep it that way.

So what's the prognosis for travel risk management? Will tracking evolve so far that travellers can tell their smart watch to 'beam me up' when in danger? I'd rather not stake my name on it – yet. What will have an earlier impact is something that looks more like *Minority Report* than *Star Trek:* self-driving cars and smart traffic, in, you guessed it, smart cities.

This is already a reality for some of us, as the first self-driving cars are being used and tested in California. Google, who's behind the self-driven car, wants to make this publicly available by 2020 (Google, n.d.) – and then it'll need a little more time to hit the car-rental market and thus impact our corporate travellers.

But to have a large impact and the best possible use from self-driving cars means large investments. For example, cities need to get 'smart' as well to enable infrastructure to work with those self-driving cars (and the odd pedestrian if there'll be any of those around then). To make this happen, the UK is launching self-driving pods in London and other cities: partly to test the concept, partly to get people accustomed to this new form of transport (Wakefield, 2016).

Smart cities are also not such a novel idea as you might think (and apologies to all those readers who already know far more than me on that topic). There are several cities around the world that have already implemented initiatives (like Southampton, UK) and are working on further projects. These include anything from parking spaces to energy consumption, health services and housing requirements.

The impact on corporate travel will be (hopefully) a much more seamless travel experience, less waiting times and more efficiency on the road – and that is something worth looking forward to.

There are, naturally, many more exciting things being developed as we speak and only time will tell how and if they'll have an impact on the industry at large. One thing is for certain, though, we'll still travel for trade, sharing knowledge, innovation and education.

Summary

This chapter has taken us through the history of corporate travel, starting with the New Kingdom of Egypt 3,500 years ago and first female pharaoh Hatshepsut. From roughly 1,500 BC to around 1900 AD, we then looked at the way travel developed as different reasons for travelling emerged.

Travelling to trade is the most basic reason. Travelling to share knowledge in an age where the importance of information (and resulting power) was uncovered. Travelling to innovate as people came together with ideas or concerns and found solutions together in traditions and by merging customs. And, finally, travelling to explore and educate, seeking knowledge for knowledge's sake – not only for the power it could bring.

Moving through the last 100 years there are some great discoveries and achievements. However, the 9/11 attacks in the US and the global economic downturn of 2008/2009 (and subsequent slow recovery) left a lasting impact on corporate travel, involving not only tighter security – but also tighter budgets.

Moving into present day and the last five years or so: what is corporate travel today? Faster travelling times, complexities in scheduling and choices of suppliers mean there are many things to consider as travel manager – and traveller. Top that up with regional, or even local, differences and you understand why corporate travel actually needs to be managed.

Looking at current topics and trends, including travel risk management, payment options and the sharing economy, the advances in technologies across industries are speeding up these developments and making us wonder what's next.

The view on corporate travel tomorrow provides some insights, largely drawn from personal experience working in the industry. Virtual collaboration is going to see its rebirth with decreased initial investments and a general better understanding of how this will help collaboration overall (and not necessarily cut travel costs).

Furthermore, wearable technologies, smarter everythings (like cars and whole cities) will bring innovation to corporate travel – that is, for the moment, possibly beyond imagination.

So before we start to lift off into space, let's get back down to the core subject and see who is involved in the business of corporate travel.

Bibliography

Advito. (2015, September). *Advito*. Accessed October 5, 2015, from Industry Forecast 2016: www.advito.com/insights/wp-advito-industry-forecast-2016/

Advito. (2015, July). *Advito*. Accessed from Advito social community playbook: www.advito.com/solutions/advito-social-community-playbook/

Ancient History Encyclopedia. (2011). *Ancient*. Accessed January 23, 2016, from Achaemenid Empire: www.ancient.eu/Achaemenid_Empire/

Appleton, D. (1862). *Annual Cyclopaedia and Register of Important Events of the year 1862*. New York: D. Appleton.

Ariely, D. (2009). *Predictably Irrational*. Harper Collins.

Baker, M. B. (2015, August 10). *BTN*. Accessed January 25, 2016, from Hertz to Cease Car Sharing Services in US: www.businesstravelnews.com/Business-Travel/Hertz-To-Cease-Car-Sharing-Services-In-U-S-Next-Month

BBC. (2014). *BBC History*. Accessed August 05, 2015, from Captain James Cook (1728 - 1779): www.bbc.co.uk/history/historic_figures/cook_captain_james.shtml

BBC. (2015, January 13). *BBC*. Accessed January 23, 2016, from The man who opened India's first call centre: www.bbc.co.uk/news/magazine-30729450

BCD Travel. (2014). *BCD Travel*. Accessed from White paper download – Total Trip Planning: www.bcdtravel.com/wp-total-trip-planning/

Bhatia, V. (2014, March 6). *Hotel News Now*. Accessed from Making the Move to Dynamic Pricing: www.hotelnewsnow.com/Article/13290

Bloy, M. (2013). *History Home*. Accessed August 06, 2015, from Railway Expansion: www.history-home.co.uk/peel/railways/expans.htm

Boston Tea Party. (2016). *Boston Tea Party Ship*. Accessed from British East India Tea Company Logo: www.bostonteapartyship.com/wp-content/themes/btps/images/british-east-india-tea-company-logo.jpg

Campbell, E. M. (2016). *Encyclopaedia Britannica*. Accessed January 23, 2016, from Giovanni Da Pian Del Carpini: www.britannica.com/biography/Giovanni-da-Pian-del-Carpini

Campbell, J. (2013, March 03). *BTN*. Accessed from Coca-Cola brings name game to Europe: www.businesstravelnews.com/Travel-Management/Coca-Cola-Brings-Name-Game-To-Europe/?a=mgmt

Cusack, M. K. (n.d.). *Everything PanAm*. Accessed January 23, 2016, from Everything PanAm: www.everythingpanam.com/

EastIndiaCompany. (2014). *The East India Company*. Accessed from The East India Company: www.theeastindiacompany.com/#

Encyclopaedia Britannica. (2015, May 05). *Encyclopaedia Britannica*. Accessed from Francesco Datini - Italian merchant and banker: www.britannica.com/biography/Francesco-Datini

Encyclopaedia Britannica. (2015). *Encyclopaedia Britannica*. Accessed from Christopher Columbus - Italian Explorer: www.britannica.com/biography/Christopher-Columbus

FedEx. (2016). *FedEx*. Accessed January 23, 2016, from History – About FedEx: about.van.fedex.com/our-story/history-timeline/history/

Forgan, S. (2000, February). A compendium of Victorian culture. *Nature, 403*(6770), 596. doi:10.1038/35001134

Fortini, A. (2015). *Slate.com*. Accessed from How the Runway Took Off: www.slate.com/articles/arts/fashion/2006/02/how_the_runway_took_off.html

GBT. (2015). *American Express - Global Business Travel*. Accessed from 100 Years of Business Travel: www.amexglobalbusinesstravel.com/100thanniversary/files/GBT100_Milestones_1915-1955.jpg

GBTA. (2015). *GBTA*. Accessed from 2016 Global Travel Price Outlook: www3.gbta.org/l/5572/2015-07-13/2k8rsp

Google. (n.d.). *Google*. Accessed from Google Self-Driving Cars: www.google.com/selfdrivingcar/

Hapag-Lloyd. (n.d.). *Hapag-Lloyd*. Accessed from Economic boom until World War II: www.hapag-lloyd.com/en/about_us/history_between_1919_1945.html

Hertz. (2015). *Hertz*. Accessed from Hertz History View: www.hertz.com/rentacar/abouthertz/index.jsp?targetPage=CorporateProfile.jsp&c=aboutHertzHistoryView

Hilton Worldwide. (2015). *Hilton Worldwide*. Accessed January 23, 2016, from History and Heritage – Hilton Worldwide: hiltonworldwide.com/about/history/

IMF. (n.d.). *International Monetary Fund*. Accessed from Cooperation and reconstruction (1944-71): www.imf.org/external/about/histcoop.htm

Iran Chamber Society. (n.d.). *Iran Chamber Society*. Accessed January 23, 2016, from History of Iran: Achaemnid Empire: www.iranchamber.com/history/achaemenids/achaemenids.php

Lienhard, J. H. (1997). *Engines of our ingenuity*. Accessed January 23, 2016, from No. 1158 – The Crystal Palace: www.uh.edu/engines/epi1158.htm

Logan, G. (2008). *USA Today*. Accessed from The effects of 9/11 on the airline industry: traveltips.usatoday.com/effects-911-airline-industry-63890.html

McAlone, N. (2015, September 13). *Tech Insider*. Accessed January 23, 2016, from Uber's history and rise to become the most valuable startup in the world: www.techinsider.io/history-of-uber-and-its-rise-to-become-the-most-valuable-startup-in-the-world-2015-9

Mcnulty, M. A. (2011, March 11). *BTN*. Accessed January 25, 2016, from Gamification in Travel Management: www.businesstravelnews.com/Travel-Management/Gamification-In-Travel-Management-Is-This-The-Next-New-Thing-To-Drive-Compliance-?a=proc

Microsoft. (2015, October). *Microsoft*. Accessed January 23, 2016, from A history of windows – Microsoft: windows.microsoft.com/en-gb/windows/history#T1=era0

National Academy of Engineering. (2015). *Great Achievements*. Accessed August 05, 2015, from Airplane Timeline: www.greatachievements.org/?id=3728

Online Archive of California. (n.d.). *OAC*. Accessed from Tillie Lewis Foods Collection: www.oac.cdlib.org/findaid/ark:/13030/tf6t1nb1s8/

Qantas. (n.d.). *Qantas*. Accessed from The Inspiration: www.qantas.com.au/travel/airlines/history-inspiration/global/en

Roerig, C. (2015). *The Metropolitan Museum of Art*. Accessed from Egypt in the New Kingdom (ca. 1550–1070 B.C.): www.metmuseum.org/TOAH/hd/nking/hd_nking.htm

Sabre. (n.d.). *Sabre*. Accessed from Our History: www.sabre.com/index.php/about/our-history

Schaal, D. (2015, June 1). *Skift*. Accessed January 25, 2016, from Hyatt invests in Onefinestay to figure out sharing economy appeal: skift.com/2015/06/01/hyatt-invests-in-onefinestay-to-figure-out-sharing-economy-appeal/

Silkroad Foundation. (2000). *Silkroad Foundation*. Accessed from Marco Polo and His Travels: p://www.silk-road.com/artl/marcopolo.shtml

Skyscanner. (2015). *Skyscanner*. Accessed from Venice to Beijing : www.skyscanner.net/transport/flights/veni/pek/150922/150926/airfares-from-venice-to-beijing-capital-in-september-2015.html?adults=1&children=0&infants=0&cabinclass=economy&rtn=1&preferdirects=false&outboundaltsenabled=false&inboundaltsenabled=false

Smithsonian. (n.d.). *Smithsonian National Air and Space Museum*. Accessed from The Wright Brothers: airandspace.si.edu/exhibitions/wright-brothers/online/

Stein, A. J. (2001, February 1). *History Link*. Accessed January 23, 2016, from www.historylink.org/index.cfm?DisplayPage=output.cfm&File_Id=1181

Swarbrooke, J., & Horner, S. (2001). *Business Travel and Tourism*. Abingdon, Great Britain: Routledge.

Talbot-Booth, E. (1936). *Ships and the Sea*. London: Sampson Low.

The Intrepid Traveler. (2013). *Travel Industry Dictionary*. Accessed from Define Corporate Travel Manager: www.travel-industry-dictionary.com/corporate-travel-manager.html

Thomas Cook. (n.d.). *Thomas Cook*. Accessed from Key Dates: www.thomascook.com/thomas-cook-history/key-dates/

Toyota. (2015). *Toyota*. Accessed from History of Toyota (1950-1959): www.toyota-global.com/company/history_of_toyota/1950-1959.html

Travel China Guide. (2015). *Travel China Guide*. Accessed January 23, 2016, from Silk Road in Tang Dynasty: www.travelchinaguide.com/silk-road/history/tang-dynasty.htm

Travelpro. (2016). *Travelpro*. Accessed January 23, 2016, from Travelpro: www.travelpro.com/history.cfm

Tuck School of Business at Dartmouth. (2011, September). *Arthur W. Page Society*. Accessed from Starbucks Coffee Company: www.awpagesociety.com/wp-content/uploads/2011/09/Starbucks-Case.pdf

Tyldesley, J. (2015). *Encyclopedia Britannica*. Accessed from Hatshepsut - Ruler of Egypt: www.britannica.com/biography/Hatshepsut

UATP. (2015, August 1). *UATP*. Accessed from UATP Forms Strategic Relationship with WEX: www.uatp.com/news-and-events/press-releases/2015/08/UATP%20Forms%20Strategic%20Relationship%20With%20WEX%20To%20Bring%20Virtual%20Credit%20Card%20Solution%20To%20The%20Market.html

Wakefield, J. (2016, January 29). *BBC*. Accessed January 30, 2016, from London's first driverless cars based on Heathrow 'pods': www.bbc.co.uk/news/technology-35432687

Webfoundation. (2015). *Webfoundation*. Accessed January 23, 2016, from History of the Web - worldwide web: webfoundation.org/about/vision/history-of-the-web/

Wikipedia. (2014). *Wikipedia*. Accessed from First voyage of James Cook: en.wikipedia.org/wiki/First_voyage_of_James_Cook

Wikipedia. (2015). *Wikipedia*. Accessed from Ellen Church: en.wikipedia.org/wiki/Ellen_Church

Wikipedia. (2015). *Wikipedia*. Accessed from Chicago Railroad Fair: en.wikipedia.org/wiki/Chicago_Railroad_Fair

Wikipedia. (2016). *Wikipedia*. Accessed January 23, 2016, from 1964 New York World's Fair - Wikipedia: en.wikipedia.org/wiki/1964_New_York_World%27s_Fair

Wikipedia. (2016, January 22). *Wikipedia*. Accessed January 23, 2016, from Skype - Wikipedia: en.wikipedia.org/wiki/Skype#History

CHAPTER 3

Who is Who in Corporate Travel

By the end of this chapter you'll be able to:

✓ Know who the key stakeholders are, what they do and how they add value to the industry.

✓ Have insights into other stakeholders that may be passively involved or have an impact on education.

✓ Develop an understanding of the many different roles and responsibilities in the corporate travel industry.

Quick Facts

♦ Corporate travel managers have many roles to play in their day-to-day lives; from communication expert to negotiation wizard, everything is possible – and needed.

♦ Travel Management Companies (TMCs) are a cornerstone of the corporate travel industry, providing advice and actions to travel managers – including booking travel arrangements.

♦ The big three travel suppliers are airlines, hotels and car rental companies. But there are many other players in this space.

♦ Not everyone is in it for their own sake; associations provide valuable insights to competitors, aiming to share information and educate the industry.

Introduction

This chapter introduces the stakeholders in corporate travel: the travel manager, travel management companies (TMCs), travel suppliers (such as airlines and hotels) and others that play a role today (consultants, the global distribution system providers, associations as body of knowledge for the industry – and the travellers themselves).

The last chapter on the history and current situation of corporate travel already introduced some of the challenges all stakeholders face in the industry:

- Everything is faster
- Multiple choices
- Complexities of systems and tools
- Duty of care
- Tight budgets

The travel manager has also already been singled out for their sometimes unpopular role of keeping travellers compliant and enforcing (strict) travel rules. But what do they do on a daily basis? Are there differences in work routines from large corporations to small and medium enterprises (SMEs)? And how do travel managers engage with the other stakeholders? That's the beginning of this chapter and it lays the groundwork for the following parts about travel policy, sourcing, operations and – eventually – the trip cycle.

Moving on from the complexities of the role of the travel manager, we'll look at the next stakeholder: the travel management company (TMC). They provide support, guidance, tools and (wo)manpower to travel managers to fulfil the travel programme. We'll take a look at the global TMCs and discuss whether or not it's a good thing to have one company service travel globally, or if local solutions might provide better value.

From there we move on to the travel suppliers: airlines, hotel chains and car-rental companies. What does it mean to corporate travel when either of these suppliers merge with another one? What are their distribution channels and what are they looking to change? There's a lot to be said in this part because it's dealing with the multiple-choices problem discussed earlier.

Finally, we take a look at other players who have a part in corporate travel, but aren't interacting quite as frequently as the aforementioned groups. The global distribution systems kick this section off: while needed daily, interaction with them as stakeholders is limited. Then it's the consultants, those people who provide extra insights or expertise to a specific topic for a travel manager. Onto the associations, some of which have already been named previously, but how do they fit in and what is their role as educators? And finally, the stakeholder you might have considered first: the traveller. All this circus is created for this one traveller at a time, yet her importance as a stakeholder is somewhat limited.

The Travel Manager

The travel manager, also referred to as corporate travel manager, has many hats to wear, as they're dealing with many different tasks. They have to be salespeople to 'sell' the travel programme to their travellers, they have to be in charge of procurement, getting the best deals from suppliers, they have to be marketers to win support and buy in from important stakeholders, they have to be police officers, security managers, concierges, money-savers, news broadcasters and the list goes on.

So let's look at their tasks and responsibilities in more detail, the challenges they face and the way they engage with internal and external stakeholders.

Role of the Travel Manager

Before jumping into the more gritty day-to-day responsibilities, the following provides an overview of the travel manager's definition and of the role they play in their organisation.

> *A middle management position. Corporate travel managers are tasked with setting corporate travel policy and standardizing and overseeing all travel by corporate employees on company business. Many corporate travel managers function as in-house travel agents.*
>
> *(The Intrepid Traveler 2013)*

Even in these few lines of the definition, there's plenty of tasks mentioned already:

- Setting corporate travel policy
- Standardising all travel
- Overseeing all travel by corporate employees on business
- In-house travel agent

Note that it's customary in small firms for corporate travel managers to also take on the role of travel agent. In larger corporations this is generally outsourced to an online solution (like Expedia) or to a travel management company (TMC) – but more of those later.

The above list comprises a full-time job: setting policy, standardising travel and overseeing bookings made on behalf of the company – keeping everything aligned – and this is no mean task. But now take a look at the next page, outlining the responsibilities of an actual job posting for a corporate travel manager on Reed.co.uk.

Job Responsibilities of a Corporate Travel Manager (Evolve Recruitment 2015)

RESPONSIBILITIES:

- Work closely with vendors, tool suppliers and other stakeholder groups to manage, deploy and implement the strategy and the programmes

- Ensure strategic meeting management process is adhered to under Travel and Meetings Policy guidelines, including reporting violations to higher management

- Track and reconcile event and travel spend to ensure adherence to event budget and monitor volume for room nights, meeting rooms and entire spend as required to provide a source of information to secure additional savings based on usage together with preferred suppliers and Procurement

- Strong collaboration with Regional Travel Leads, Procurement and IT Business partner

- Utilise technology to oversee usage of the respective programmes and run extensive reports

- Ensure that all partners are researching and booking economically feasible rates for all aspects of employee lodging and travel for offsite meetings

- Provide excellent management of suppliers and supervision of individuals responsible for meeting and events

- Interact with the leadership of the organisation, adapt best practices and provide best in class service

- Maintain current knowledge of industry trends and information to be able to offer new ideas to internal customers to better meet their needs

- Track savings on meetings achieved through strategic meeting management process

- Understand and adhere to the company's risk and regulatory standards, policies and controls in accordance with the company´s risk management guidelines

- Identify risk-related issues needing escalation to management

- Resolve problems or complaints from consultants both internal and external as related to meetings and events

- Oversight of the issuance and cancellation of centrally held cards, maintenance of organisational hierarchy, and production of management reporting

- Monitor and report on key performance metrics related to exception/non-compliance reporting

- Monitor spending for compliance to policy, works with supplier to minimise credit losses and to identify financial risk factors while working with stakeholders to resolve issues

- Liaise with ETS Finance / Expense Accounting to ensure policies and procedures are aligned, integration with Expense system is optimized, help desk teams are briefed to answer employee questions, and cardholders receive appropriate support for escalation issues

- Create and manage documentation policy, procedures and communications to establish global standards and support implementation of best practices

- Create communications and maintain intranet information to assist cardholders to manage their accounts effectively and delivers customer service to the business

- Oversee help desk structure and contracted employees from the card supplier (responsible for administrative tasks related to the programme)

- Responsible for special card related projects as needed by Global Travel programme

How does that sound? Are you willing to apply for the post?

Naturally, not all these tasks happen on a daily basis. But it's crucial that none of them are forgotten when focussing on, for example, the travel policy. Here the travel manager needs to bring all those elements together and show her true skills in finding the best possible solution for all involved:

- Saving money for the company
- Organising adequate travel options for employees
- Ensuring safety and security for all travellers
- Creating reporting to track and audit
- Bringing business to preferred suppliers

These are looked at more closely in chapter four under travel policy and operations, so let's turn our attention to the second part of the job description. The skills, experience and knowledge the travel manager needs to perform these tasks.

The list on the following page is from the same job description, and at a glance you notice that, while there are a lot of skills on there, none really stands out as 'very difficult' or 'specialist'.

Job skills needed for a Corporate Travel Manager position (Evolve Recruitment 2015)

- Skills, Experience and Knowledge
- Bachelor's degree (or equivalent)
- First-hand experience in a service environment or travel management function
- Ideally experience in running both a meetings and event function or a card programme
- Excellent written and oral communication skills
- Interpersonal and intercultural competences
- Presentation skills
- Highly organised
- Ability to prioritise main duties
- Problem-solving capacity
- Multi-tasking abilities
- Team worker
- Negotiation competences
- Computer skills
- Attention to detail
- Able to work under stress
- Able to work without close supervision
- Self-motivated, creative and initiative
- Accountability and responsibility
- Growth mindset
- Consumer and customer focus
- Bias for action
- Building talent and teams

Often, travel managers are hired from travel agencies – switching sides, so to speak. In that case, they have a vast background in everything travel-related, but not much expertise in the running of a business or strategy. On the other hand, when the new travel manager comes from a business background, they often don't understand the corporate travel industry completely.

Differences in Corporations

Before talking about challenges travel managers face, let's first discuss differences of companies who employ them. And as you'll see below, it's not only size that matters.

Large Corporations

In large corporations, chances are you won't only have one travel manager, but several – and often across the globe. Large companies are those that appear on the Fortune 500 index, and in travel it's common to talk about large companies when they spend over $12 million on air travel alone (Boehmer 2014).

As a reminder, the BTN Corporate 100 Index looks at the biggest spenders in corporate travel on air volume in the US, with IBM leading the 2014 list at $590 million. Stand alone, this looks like a very large figure to 'just' be spending on air travel, so let's put this into context: in the same year, IBM published revenue of more than $92 billion (IBM 2015); that means US air travel spending equals less than 1% of revenues.

Back to the travel manager in large corporations: there'll be a hierarchy of course, with one person responsible for global travel management and direct reports in the regions and additional resources to help on certain parts of the travel programme.

You'll also often find this part of travel management outsourced to a TMC whereby the employees of that TMC are working as employees within the corporation.

Small & Medium Corporations

As travel manager in a small or medium corporation you're looking at between $2 million and $12 million for medium companies and everything that has air-travel volumes below $2 million is considered small (Boehmer 2014).

There are two major differences for travel managers: smaller teams, meaning less resources available to run the travel programme, and a tendency to work more independently of TMCs as so-called 'unmanaged accounts' or working solely via online agencies.

Not for Profit Organisations

A number of organisations also have the need for travel management and best rates in order to help others: charities, for example. They also have travel managers in place, and some of them, in 2013, created a platform called FORE to bring them together – and use that joined power for supplier negotiations (Boehmer 2015).

With this approach, they've already created a 'large corporation' with annual air-spend of more than $100 million (FORE 2015). Not all services are bought through this consortium, as some deals are already in place and work well – but in future there's ambition to grow and extend the collaboration in travel management.

Challenges for the Travel Manager

We already looked at some challenges travel managers face with their travellers in chapter two:

- Duty of care
- Negotiated rates and compliance
- Lost opportunities
- Data availability

But travel managers aren't alone; TMCs and suppliers share some of the pain as they're dependent on the bookings through compliant channels and data availability. Furthermore, they help travel managers look after travellers on the road and are vital in providing duty of care information (more about that in chapter four).

There are, however, some challenges that are inbred into the industry. With more understanding about corporate travel and its importance to the company and the company's strategy, I hope that one day these challenges will be overcome. They stem mainly from too little senior management support (or even buy in).

As we found out earlier, travel accounts for about 2% of a company's revenues. Hence, the travel manager is often side-lined, finding it hard to make senior executives appreciate the many facets of the role. This, in turn, leads to the following challenges.

Demand Management

This refers to the travel manager's ability to influence the number of trips booked. Naturally, this equals zero: the travel manager doesn't have the information, data or relationships with other departments to find out (amongst others):

- The number of trips necessary
- Who needs to travel
- Who might be optional
- Who could stay a day longer and cover something else so that only one trip suffices

Behaviour Management

The travel manager's ability to influence how trips are planned, when they are booked, how much it costs and which suppliers are used is labelled behaviour management.

It's easier than demand management, because here the travel manager deals directly with travellers. And there's a travel programme and policy that everyone should adhere to, so there's already a platform to influence behaviour. But it's not quite as simple as that.

Influencing behaviour requires a lot of effort and patience. It's all about communication and engaging travellers. Behaviour management is about making them feel they are stakeholders in their travel programme – and, therefore, making them accountable to what they've created.

Performance Measurements

This refers to how the travel manager's performance is rated at the end of the year. It's what's known as 'paper savings': travel figures are estimated on paper for the following year, based somewhat on previous years. Then a percentage saving, let's say 5%, is applied across the travel programme, which the travel manager has to achieve.

The travel manager then negotiates with the suppliers based on the estimates – and the savings target. Once the contracts are in place, the travel manager has 'achieved' the goal. But still, only on paper.

With data becoming more easily and readily available, now is the time for travel managers to push for using actual travel data rather than approximations. This will make the whole travel management process much more transparent – and every stakeholder more accountable.

Engaging with Stakeholders

Now that you know how difficult it is to be a travel manager, let me make sure you're aware of the fun side as well.

As travel manager you're very, very popular at all sorts of industry events. To many conferences you can go free of charge, participating in so-called hosted-buyer programmes.

While it's nice to be the centre of attention, it can be a bit daunting if you have the feeling people are only talking to you because you might buy something from them. But don't worry, there aren't that many conferences in the year.

Travel managers ideally should have a trusting relationship with their account manager at the TMC (if the corporation is large enough to have a TMC, that is). They provide helpful guidance and can keep travel managers updated with industry developments.

Another source for comfort and information (sharing) are the associations: ACTE (Association of Corporate Travel Executives) and GBTA (Global Business Travel Association). Note that these are the two global representations, but there are many others more localised. They often have a partnership with one or other of the global associations in place.

Examples of local organisations are:

- ITM (Institute of Travel and Meetings) in the UK
- VDR (Verband Deutscher Reisebueros) in Germany
- DBTA (Danish Business Travel Association) in Denmark

Let's now have a look at these other stakeholders and their roles in corporate travel.

> Hosted-buyer programmes offer free-of-charge conference places for travel buyers in return for meeting suppliers at pre-arranged times.

The Travel Management Company (TMC)

The TMC found its purpose in helping corporations with their travel requests. They started very much like your everyday travel agency, except they'd serve companies only. And even today most of the employees are agents helping travellers on the phone with their arrangements. But in this part the focus is more on the supporting departments and the shift of focus for the TMC.

The Role of the TMC

While arranging travel for corporates lies at the heart of the TMC, technological advances and new business models have introduced changes. On one hand it opened up opportunities to broaden their services on offer; on the other hand, it put a 'best-by date' on services that are fading out.

Traditionally, the business model of the TMC was to earn a commission from the suppliers whose services they sold to the travellers. But when in 2002 airlines started scrapping commissions, the TMCs had to change. Their core offerings now are sourcing suppliers (from airlines to parking and even video-conferencing facilities), supporting the creation of travel policies and travel programmes and providing the clients with management information on a range of travel-related subjects (from cost savings to CO_2 emissions).

Here is one company's definition of corporate business travel management (Management Solutions UK Ltd 2015):

> *The process of optimising the business travel spend, taking out excess, reducing processing costs and keeping your travellers happy and satisfied in the process by delivering an efficient, cost effective and expert service.*

> *A more standard definition, not coming from a company trying to sell its services, is:*

> *'Travel Management Company: A travel agency that serves mainly business accounts. Typically provides both online and offline reservation fulfilment, access to data and reporting, traveller tracking, consulting, benchmarking and negotiation services.'*

(BTN 2015)

More recently, TMCs are also exploring ways of developing relationships directly with travellers to build loyalty and brand awareness.

One of the global TMCs, BCD Travel, came up with a graphical way to showcase all the many services and products a travel-management company deals with (BCD Travel 2015). This is based on the following categories:

- Planning and en-route services
- Intelligence and analytics
- Travel risk management

- Demand and behaviour management
- Payment and expense management
- Programme support and optimisation

This is just a little reminder of the complex industry corporate travel has become in recent years; the graphic used to be shown as an underground network to show the connections between the different categories. However, since there are so many connections and nothing really is in isolation anymore, the layout had to change to something more simplistic (as seen in Figure 1).

Figure 1: BCD Travel Solutions

Departments of the TMC

Now that you have an overview of all the services the TMC supplies, let's have a look at some of the departments and their functions in a little more detail.

Business Development and Sales

These are the people who look for new business opportunities. They are the first point of contact for a company in need for managed travel, and thus are the 'face' of the company. It's up to them to start and foster relationships – even if business opportunities are still far off.

In general, contracts with travel-management companies are done for a number of years (anything between three and five) because of the complex negotiations and implementations that follow a decision on such a scale. Hence, business developers often start talking to travel managers who 'don't go out to bid' for another two years.

The process of hiring a TMC is a lengthy one that's started by a company asking several TMCs to be part of an RFP (request for proposal). This is a longwinded questionnaire TMCs have to answer and is followed by a number of presentations and discussions. The process takes easily a year (or longer) to complete.

Account Management

Account managers have an important role: on a daily basis to advise and support the travel manager, but also to keep the client engaged and satisfied with the services so they won't start a new bidding process at the end of the contract.

As everything else in travel, even account management can get quite complex. There are account managers looking after multiple smaller and mid-size companies and there are multiple account managers looking after large, multi-national corporations. In the latter case there's generally one global account manager in place (just like on the corporation's side there would be one global travel manager), who has direct reports of regional and local account managers servicing a client.

The race for new business is ongoing, which is why account managers' efforts to retain an account are an important part of their role. During the service agreement term, any unsatisfactory performance should be flagged and amended as soon as possible. It should also be recorded and solutions discussed on a global level because it's often the ability of TMCs to react to problems and communicate with the travel manager that decides whether or not the engagement continues in the future.

Supplier Relations

This department is an important link between the clients of the TMC and the suppliers. And because of that, they have different tasks to perform. In part, they're account managers, maintaining good relationship with suppliers through regular meetings, reviews and collaboration projects.

Another part of their work is around negotiations. TMCs not only help their clients to obtain negotiated deals with suppliers, they generally also have preferred rates in place with air and hotel providers. These rates are used for clients who don't have enough volume to negotiate their own deals and, naturally, for the TMC travel arrangements, as well.

Marketing

There are two particular streams of marketing within a TMC: one side deals with the general day-to-day marketing of the company, maintaining websites and social media, arranging speaking engagements, publishing press releases, aligning the brand across the globe and making sure everything comes across as one brand – thereby strengthening the corporate identity of the TMC.

The other side deals with product marketing. People working here are closely engaged with the product development and research teams and provide collateral for the public and (almost more importantly) provide training and more in-depth information on new products and services for the commercial teams (i.e. business development, sales and account management).

Naturally the two parts of marketing work closely together to ensure the TMC's brand is coherent in both internal and external environments.

Product Development & Research

These are the people working on the 'next big thing' in business travel. They watch trends emerge and conduct studies around feasibility and impact – as well as the value this might bring to travel managers.

In the early stages, when the industry is talking about new topics, it's the research teams that set out to find out more. For example, when Uber and Airbnb started to have a larger imprint on leisure travel, BCD Travel's research team compiled a white paper to educate their clients on what this might mean for their travel programme. The research team gathers data, information and possibly even clients who want to try and test a new solution before it gets to market (naturally, they get preferential treatment for their guinea-pig role).

As stated, white papers are also produced in these teams as they help the industry as a whole to cope with new topics. From experience it takes about one to two years for the industry to buy into a new product, even on a topic that's been highly visible in the media and much discussed at events – like the sharing economy.

In later stages, it's the product-development team that decides which products are ready to move to the next stage (i.e. launch) and which are not providing an added advantage over the competition – in other words, aren't likely to bring more clients and/or money to the TMC. It's a high-pressure environment in which teams have to continuously scan information and gauge whether hypes make the full conversion to a trend.

A good example is the sharing economy discussed earlier. When it started out it was deemed to be only a solution for leisure travellers and that the complex demands of corporates wouldn't want anything to do with it. The TMCs still looked into the subject and providers of sharing-economy services pushed into the corporate space altering their offering to meet their criteria. While sharing-economy services aren't completely mainstream yet, suppliers have seen a niche and jumped in. It's now up to the product development teams to get their portfolios aligned to match client needs.

Naturally, there are many other departments like human resources, finance, IT, security, and those supporting the ones mentioned above. To write about them all would fill another book and will have to wait for another day.

The Global TMCs

Throughout this book there have already been references to the global TMCs that are the main players today: American Express Global Business Travel, Carlson Wagonlit Travel and BCD Travel.

There are, of course, many others, both on a global and on regional and local scales but to mention them all is (again) out of scope.

American Express Global Business Travel (Amex GBT)

The largest player in the industry, not only in terms of annual revenues but also as representing most of the Corporate 100 companies (i.e. 37) surveyed in the BTN Index (West 2015).

Having the power of the credit cards and payment solutions at their back, they've created a TMC powerhouse. On their website they describe their services like this:

> *'Our corporate travel management offers a strategic approach to your travel program. We can help you navigate booking compliance, cost allocation and mobile itinerary. Your Travelers deserve responsive and comprehensive support – when crises arise our corporate travel management services can help your employees get home safely. Our Travel Counsellors and Client Managers offer personalized attention to both your Travelers and your corporate travel management program.'*

(American Express Global Business Travel 2015)

Amex GBT doesn't disclose its revenue because of restructuring its business travel business in 2014. It provides travel management services in close to 140 countries worldwide.

Carlson Wagonlit Travel (CWT)

This privately owned company is TMC to 20 companies in the BTN Corporate 100 index. But with its specialist offering in the energy, resources and marine sector, it's tapping into a market largely unexplored by the other big TMCs.

Its description of business travel starts with the travellers, rather than with the corporations or travel managers. As mentioned earlier, the race to build relations with the actual travellers has heated up lately with the advent of TMC apps.

> *'Business travel is a key driver for getting things done. However, its effectiveness is dependent on travellers receiving the support they need to be productive and safe during their trips, and on travel buyers having access to information and tools to quickly adapt to ever-evolving internal and external dynamics. That's why CWT organizes itself around Traveller Services and Program Services, with a variety of products and services tailored to the specific needs of each. We also offer specialized travel services to the dedicated sector of Energy, Resources & Marine.'*

(Carlson Wagonlit Travel 2015)

CWT is stating revenues of $27.3 billion in its 'at a glance' section for 2014 and is represented in 150 countries and territories worldwide (Carlson Wagonlit Travel 2015).

BCD Travel

In case you were wondering why the abbreviation BCD hasn't been explained yet, it's not an abbreviation. The story goes that ABC was already taken as a business name (didn't google research that at all?) and the next logical thought was to go with 'BCD'.

It's very well represented in the BTN Corporate 100 index, servicing 23 clients on the list.

'On the surface, corporate travel seems straightforward—get employees where they need to go for business. But we help you look below the surface so you can find opportunities to turn your travel program into the most simplified, streamlined, cost-effective, tweet-worthy experience for travellers and management alike.'

(BCD Travel 2015)

One thing BCD Travel is very good at is calling out the complexities, thereby acknowledging travel managers' 'pain points' (frustration) at not being taken seriously when they try to explain that it's not as simple as getting someone from A to B.

BCD Travel recorded revenues of $24.2 billion in 2014 and services 110 countries around the world. It is, like CWT, a privately owned company with head offices located in the Netherlands (BCD Travel 2015).

Future of TMCs

Before we make our way to the travel suppliers and other stakeholders, let's briefly discuss the future of travel management companies.

As stated in the introduction to this part, technology advances and business model changes have already shaped the TMC of today. But there are more developments underway and with the growing service platform of the internet, the question arises whether the TMC might soon be a thing of the past?

TMCs have traditionally supported companies to keep their travel services and needs tightly knitted together. Often they bundle services to provide for the many travellers at the same time. It's an approach for the masses rather than the individual; but due to personalisation of services in private lives, travel managers are starting to expect a more tailored approach to the management of their travel programme as well.

There's also the data side to consider. In the past it was very difficult to find out what one trip actually costs the company. There's not only the booking information to consider, which might give the dollar amounts for the air ticket and the hotel accommodation, but also the on-trip expenses: meals, entertaining clients, coffee, taxis and other ground transportation, WiFi, exchange rates and many more. These are captured through credit-card bills, supplier invoices and expense reports.

The TMC is in a great place to offer multi-source data consolidation, and they already do – but it's slow-going. Data is not standardised across channels, and so far there's a lot of human input required to even start the analysis. But there's hope that new capabilities of looking at data and advances in machine learning might be deployed in future to speed up the process and then drive better decisions.

However, the model of calling an agent to book a trip are likely soon to be over. At the moment, it's the more complex trips that still need human interaction: either a multi-stop trip with flexible dates, or a trip to an 'out-of-the-way' location.

Whichever way you look at it, the TMC's current business model will have to adapt to changes in booking behaviour, consumption and reliance on data, and the request for personal attention.

The Travel Suppliers

One can argue, of course, that the TMCs are travel suppliers, but seeing that they play such an important part in corporate travel and have a very unique role, they have got an extra section devoted to them.

Traditionally, corporate travel looks at four core suppliers: airlines, hotels, car rental and rail. These are the big spend areas, air transactions leading the way with about 45% of all travel spend. Hotel accounts for about 20%, car rental for about 5% and rail for about 4% (BCD Travel 2013).

This still leaves over 25% unaccounted for: dining and entertainment, other ground transportation (like taxis) and mobile charges fall into this category. These are less easy to manage or negotiate contracts for, but new products, like Uber or Dinova, are helping to pave the way.

Travel Supply: Air

Air tickets are the undisputed biggest spend category of corporate travel. Hence, you often hear people refer to air spend when discussing their travel programmes. This gives everyone in the industry a rough idea of how much overall is spent on travel and how large the company is.

Air travel is supplied by airlines – through global distribution systems (we'll discuss those a little further on in this chapter). There are currently two types of air suppliers available: the legacy carriers (traditional, full-service, often national, airlines, like British Airways) and the low cost carriers (LCCs, like easyJet or Ryanair).

There's some discussion around a third type emerging: a hybrid carrier. This could either be a legacy carrier deciding to unbundle all services and charge extra or a low-cost carrier deciding to bundle some services together for extra convenience.

Legacy Carriers

In the last chapter we discussed the history of corporate travel and found that some carriers from the 1920s (like KLM and Qantas) are still in operation today. These airlines are also often referred to as full-service carriers.

The term 'legacy carriers' was coined in the US in 1978 to describe airlines with an established interstate route network in place before the Airline Deregulation Act (Wikipedia 2015). However, the term has been broadened since, and the industry at large uses it to describe full-service airlines. That's all those offering first and/or business class seating, frequent flyer programmes, access to airport lounges and often inflight entertainment (like meals and movies).

Traditionally, corporate travellers use these legacy carriers on their trips, and travel managers negotiate contracts with them. Often this goes hand-in-hand with choosing airlines belonging to the same alliance to ensure best possible connections.

The table on the following page shows a ranking of 21 airlines that made it on the Forbes 'The World's Biggest Public Companies List – 2015 Ranking' (Forbes 2015). While dominated by the legacy carriers, some low-cost carriers are represented as well.

Note that some names might be unfamiliar to you, like International Airlines Group (IAG) which comprises of British Airways, Iberia, and Vueling. Note also that there's been a lot of recent activities around mergers and acquisitions – the latest being IAG buying a 25% stake in AerLingus in August 2015 (Newcombe 2015).

Company	Country	Sales	Profit
Delta Air Lines	United States	$40.3 B	$659 M
Deutsche Lufthansa	Germany	$39.8 B	$73 M
United Continental Holdings	United States	$38.9 B	$1.1 B
Air France-KLM	France	$33.1 B	$-263M
International Airlines Group	United Kingdom	$26.7 B	$1.3B
Southwest Airlines	United States	$18.6 B	$1.1 B
China Southern Airlines	China	$17.7 B	$288 M
All Nippon Airways	Japan	$15.9 B	$358 M
China Eastern Airlines	China	$14.6 B	$554 M
Cathay Pacific Airways	Hong Kong	$13.7 B	$406 M
Singapore Airlines	Singapore	$12.1 B	$280 M
Latam Airlines	Chile	$12.1 B	$-103 M
Air Canada	Canada	$12 B	$91 M
Korean Air	South Korea	$11.3 B	$-456 M
Turkish Airlines	Turkey	$11 B	$832 M
EasyJet	United Kingdom	$7.5 B	$745 M
Ryanair Holdings	Ireland	$7.3 B	$1.1 B
Hainan Airlines	China	$5.8 B	$420 M
Alaska Air Group	United States	$5.4 B	$605 M

Biggest Airline Groups 2015

Low-Cost Carriers

The LCCs originated in the US with Southwest Airlines being the first successful carrier. On the Forbes ranking they're in sixth place.

LCCs are also often referred to as no-frills airlines, discount or budget carriers. They generally offer less comforts, although some items can be bought in addition to the airfare (luggage, on-board meals, fast boarding, etc.).

Another differentiator is that they're often flying to secondary airports. Ryanair is the best example: when you ask for a flight from London, UK, to Frankfurt, Germany, it gives you the option to fly from Luton, UK to Frankfurt-Hahn, Germany (about 120km away from Frankfurt's city centre). As a traveller, it's a good idea to plan extra time for getting to and from the airport using LCCs.

On stage at the GBTA Europe Conference in November 2014, Michael O'Leary, CEO of Ryanair, explained how he wanted to change travellers' behaviour with the low-cost approach. By charging for baggage, for example, he wanted travellers to travel light. Why? Airport charges for service desks and luggage handling are high.

As already stated, corporate travellers traditionally travel on legacy carriers. So why are we talking about LCCs here? Is it just because they are another form of travelling? Not quite: in recent years, all LCCs have made efforts to attract the corporate segment. They've introduced preferred seating, preferred check-in, some lounge access, and even something akin to a frequent-flyer programme – all that at a cost, of course.

To sum up, let's have a look at another table describing the differences between legacy (full-service) carriers and low-cost carriers (O'Connel and Willams 2005).

GET YOUR TERMS RIGHT:

Domestic – travel within one country.
Regional – travel within a region.
Intra-continental – travel within a continent.
Inter-continental – travel across continents.

Characteristic	Low-cost carrier	Full-service carrier
Brand	One brand: low pricing	Extended brand: price and service
Price	Simple pricing structure	Complex pricing structure
Distribution	Internet, direct booking	Internet, direct, and travel organisation
Checking in	No ticket	No ticket, IATA ticket contract
Airport	Mostly secondary	Primary
Network	Point-to-point	Hub-and-spoke
Classes	One class	Multiple classes
During flight	Unbundling (pay for 'extras')	Bundling (free 'extras')
Aircraft usage	Very intensive	Average - intensive
Aircraft type	One type	Multiple types
Turnaround times	25 minutes	Slow: congestion/work
Product	One product	Multiple integrated products
Secondary revenue	Advertisement, on-board selling	Focused on primary product
Seating	Tight, no reservations	Flexible, reservations
Customer service	Overall bad	Reliable service
Operational activities	Outsourcing (focused on flying)	Extending (maintenance, cargo)
Target group	Mostly tourists	Tourist and business

Comparison of LCCs to Legacy Carriers

Trends in Air Supply

Legacy carriers, worried about the success of LCCs, are increasingly unbundling services and charging extra. For example, on domestic trips in the US it's now customary to charge check–in luggage fees. European carriers are eyeing the idea and are introducing hand–luggage–only fares.

Another trend is NDC, as discussed in the previous chapter. This new distribution is going to have an impact on corporate travel but it's currently not fully rolled–out nor functional. The big worry is, though, that airlines determine prices based on the value of the travellers (i.e. the more you travel, the better your status, the better your score – and the lower your airfare). It's feared that this is a move against more transparency – something corporates are fighting for.

Something off the beaten track, which is already having some impact on the aviation industry, are drones. There have been a number of sightings, near-collisions and airport closures because of safety concerns for travellers. At a time when drones are becoming increasingly popular and usable by everyone, it's only a matter of time when tougher laws will be put in place to keep people and travellers safe (IATA 2015).

Keeping an eye on the industry, travel managers can increase their negotiation power. For example, in India many new LCCs are entering the market; this has a dampening effect on fares as competitors try to gain market share.

Travel Supply: Hotel

Hotel spend accounts for roughly 20% of overall corporate travel spend. But with a highly fragmented market, it's much more difficult to manage than airlines. That's partly because there's no standardising body (airlines have IATA) and partly because there's just so much more variety to choose from. Hotels are generally classified by star-ratings. This works well in a given market, but can be more difficult across countries or regions. That's why a tiered (text-based) approach has been introduced to ensure standards across accommodation.

Distribution for corporate travel is largely done through the GDS, but unfortunately, travellers have a record for not booking hotels through corporate channels. They like to book those hotels they have loyalty accounts with, or those they've stayed at before and know they'll get a nice room by just ringing them up.

Hotel Types and Brands

Similarly to airlines, there's two distinctive types of hotel supply: chain and independent. Chain hotels are the big names, like Hilton, Marriot and Accor. Independent hotels are lesser known and, because of that, often become part of marketing and sales organisations, like Preferred Hotels or Worldhotels.

A lot of the corporate travel volume goes into chain hotels. Travellers know what to expect when they stay here and can rely on a number of amenities and services. But there's a growing interest in less traditional accommodation: boutique and life-style hotels are quite popular and Airbnb has its own following.

So do you know your brands from your chains? Let's have a look at the Intercontinental Hotel Group (IHG – not to be confused with the international airlines group IAG mentioned above). While you might not have heard of IHG, you're sure to be familiar with its brands as shown in the table on the next page (IHG 2015). It depicts current hotels by number of properties and number of rooms. The table also shows the property pipeline, that is, hotels that are planning to come onto the market relatively soon.

Note that most chain-hotel business is run by franchising; the brand owner doesn't necessarily own the hotel, but sells the brand for marketing and increasing sales.

IHG Brand	Current Hotels		Hotel Pipeline
	Hotels	Rooms	Hotels
InterContinental	180	61,197	52
Kimpton Hotels & Restaurants	66	11,990	15
HUALUXE	2	563	23
Crowne Plaza	401	111,917	89
Hotel Indigo	62	6,919	64
EVEN	2	296	4
Holiday Inn	1,148	208,609	255
Holiday Inn Express	2,391	231,849	557
Holiday Inn Resort	45	10,742	18
Holiday Inn Club Vacations	12	4,027	1
Staybridge Suites	216	23,536	106
Candlewood Suites	330	31,402	92
Other	87	20,971	17
Total	**4,942**	**724,018**	**1,293**

IHG Brands

Star Rating

As stated above, star ratings are an important way for hotels to indicate their quality. For example, in Germany there's an organisation that grades hotels and other accommodation options by assigning stars (from 1, meaning basic, to 5, meaning luxury) based on a long list of criteria. It's called DEHOGA, an abbreviation for Deutscher Hotel- und Gaststättenverband (German hotel and public house association) and operates country-wide (DEHOGA Bundesverband n.d.).

But what about different countries? And different criteria? Or different numbers (and meanings) of stars? Take France, as another example, where star-rating stops at four. Or Dubai, where star-rating goes up to seven. And that's looking at just three countries!

To overcome this difficulty, the industry has thought up another way of rating hotels: a tiered approach. Instead of assigning stars, a text-based rating is applied ranging from 'economy' to 'luxury'. Hotel research company STR Global lists the following (STR Global 2015):

- Luxury
- Upper Upscale
- Upscale
- Upper Midscale
- Midscale
- Economy
- Independent

Independent is an extra category and though it does appear at the bottom of the list, you shouldn't expect them to be the least luxurious.

This way of classifying hotels makes it a little easier to compare 'apples with apples' for travel managers looking to extend or change their hotel programme.

Using a tiered-based approach to rating hotels has proven to be successful, but, like everything else, it's not a fool-proof method: sometimes hotels classify themselves differently than independent organisations would rate them, leading to misconceptions and possible errors in the database.

Trends in Hotel Supply

Distribution is a hotly discussed topic at the moment. Airlines are looking at NDC and selling direct to travellers, as mentioned above, and hotels, too, are on the lookout to become smarter about yield management.

Traditionally, hotels offer negotiated ('neg') rates to their corporate clients. These are valid for an agreed amount of time (usually a year) based on some criteria (availability, day of the week, events). However, hotels are increasing their number of black-out dates: days when corporate rates aren't available and the BAR (best available rate) is applied to a booking.

Currently, hotels are pushing for a shift in contracts; instead of negotiating rates, they want to negotiate discount percentages on the BAR. The BAR is calculated based on demand and availability for a set date so it can be either very high or very low – and, of course, in the middle. Travel managers are somewhat reluctant about this approach, because it's harder to budget, although there are some benefits to be had, especially in secondary cities where demand is generally lower.

YIELD MANAGEMENT:

The practice of airlines, hotels, and car-rental companies of manipulating the supply and price of their inventory to achieve maximum revenue. Also referred to as Revenue Management.

Another trend to watch is the sharing economy. We've already discussed Airbnb above, but note that more and more hotels are taking ownership in these kind of companies. They're also going to look into developing their existing products of long-stay apartments to make them more appealing to corporate travellers.

Something further down the pipeline might be holographic rooms. It's been proven that many people don't sleep well away from home. This new technology could project one's own bedroom into the hotel room. It's hoped that this would increase comfort, but more importantly, allow travellers to truly relax and wake up refreshed in the morning.

Travel Supply: Car Rental

While car rental only accounts for about five percent of travel spend, it's still an important category. More so because it's relatively easy to manage. And together with rail, it accounts for close to 10% of overall travel spend.

There's only a few global players in the car-rental arena, but there are many more options available locally. The picture is very different for rail – every country has its own system, often nationalised, which makes it more difficult to manage globally.

To add to the complexities of managed ground transportation (excluding public transport and taxis), there are new players in the market. On-demand economy providers like Uber, but also companies providing car access by the hour, like ZipCar.

Car Rental Companies

As stated there are five global players currently in the market, though note that, similarly to hotels, they all consist of several brands. It's also a bit like alliances in the airline industry, with local rental companies feeding into the global partners. Yet, often the global car rental companies buy a stake in the local venture (or take them over completely).

Figure 2 features a world map showcasing Europcar's global presence (Europcar 2014). This is followed by a table to reference the key players and their brands; the information is taken from the relevant websites of each supplier.

Figure 2 - Europcar's World View

Company	BRANDS
Hertz	Hertz / Dollar Rent a Car / Thrifty
Enterprise Holdings	Enterprise Rent a Car / Alamo / National
Europcar	Europcar / InterRent / Car2Go
Avis	Avis / Budget Rent a Car / ZipCar
Sixt	Sixt / Drive Now

Car Rental Types

Similarly to hotels, there's a tiered approach to car rental as well. The Association of Car Rental Industry System Standards (ACRISS) established in 1989 is an interest group formed by Avis, Europcar, and Hertz. Its key aim is to 'develop standards to avoid misleading information when making a car rental booking online or via any electronic means' (ACRISS 2015).

There are some differences between Europe and North America: European car types include 'mini', as well as 'elite' cars for all types, which are superior to another model of same size. Europe's fleet does not include 'oversize' cars. The following page shows the ACRISS car rental types of North America.

North American Fleet

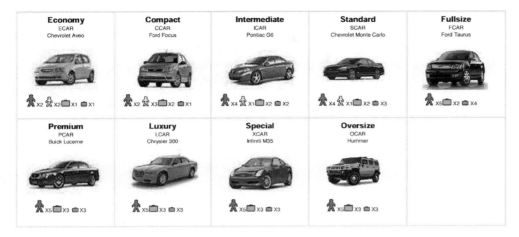

Figure 3 - Car Rental Types according to ACRISS

Note that there are some countries where it's much more common to hire a car with a driver. India and China are possibly the biggest markets where this happens – and for anyone who's ever been to these countries, chauffeur-driven cars make sense. However, as more and more people travel and infrastructure improves, it's only a matter of time when self-driving becomes a viable option.

Car Rental Business Model

The car-rental industry is fiercely competitive – even though there aren't that many global players. Since cars are the same regardless of which company rents them, suppliers have to find other ways to differentiate and obtain market share.

The most common way to do that is offering discounts and decreasing prices. And that's what they've been doing for the past few years. Every year someone in the industry will say, 'they can't go on like this, they have to raise prices this year', but so far it hasn't happened, although in 2015, car-rental companies have started to raise prices for leisure travellers.

This business model is, naturally, not sustainable. So how do companies like Hertz, Avis and co. stay in business? After all, the global car-rental industry is booming, expecting to reach $81.2 billion by 2019 (PR Newswire, 2015). They have a second income stream: selling used cars. And that's a big market! They make deals with the big auto manufacturers to take on their new cars, then, after about a year, they sell them off to people like you and me (and dealers). The upside of this is, of course, that, as a consumer of rental cars, you get very nice cars to drive.

Trends in Car Rental

Changes in this industry aren't as fast as one might expect. While bookings online and via mobile are becoming more important, they haven't had the support as seen in other industries. But things are heating up as sharing-economy providers and hybrid solutions gain steady market share (more about those just a few lines down).

Car rental is very much a traditional industry, somewhat at the mercy of auto manufacturers. It's not for them to innovate new cars – they're just the facilitators. Partly helping travellers get from A to B (and often back again), partly helping manufacturers with their marketing. The self-driving cars will be a changing point for the industry, but they're still quite a long way off.

Travel Supply: Others

There are some other players worth taking a look at – especially for those travel programmes that are already mature and seek extra savings or innovative opportunities to collaborate.

Rail

Rail is already an integral part of business travel in Europe. For domestic trips, travellers are recognising that it doesn't take a lot longer compared to air. There's also the added benefit that rail stations are generally in the middle of a city whereas airports are often on the outskirts.

Asia, Japan, China and India all have impressive rail systems and are working on improving these further. Large investments are going into these and will not only add to travel comfort, but also cut travel times by introducing high-speed trains.

The (often nationalised) operators are just starting to apply yield management, opening the doors for negotiations. Watch this space, especially as companies are getting more and more interested in CO^2 emissions and saving opportunities.

Other Ground Transport

Until the beginning of 2014 this included public transportation options and taxis. For travel managers this part of the journey is very difficult to control, because travellers are on the road and possibly not very mindful of policy.

However, this changed in July 2014 with the Uber becoming a real alternative – not just in one location. It's basically an on-demand taxi service, based on a mobile app. The traveller knows exactly where his car is and the driver knows who to pick up. There are many different Uber offerings ranging from traditional chauffeured-limousine services to true peer-to-peer sharing. For travel managers, there is extra security (when connected to the system they can see where travellers are), better reporting (Uber sends data to the company), and easier expenses (travellers can pay by card – or even automate the payment process ahead of time).

Still, taxis and public transport do exist and are often a good option for corporate travellers. There are cities and countries, for example, where Uber isn't welcome (or even banned, like in Thailand) (Business Insider, 2015). And mobiles make it possible for travel managers to interact with their travellers on the road. Common examples of influencing on-trip behaviour are sending messages upon arrival at a destination, saying 'please use public transport to get to your hotel' or 'as it's late, please use a taxi'.

Other Accommodation

Another very young company is making headlines around the world: Airbnb. Started in 2008, the company is now operative in over 190 countries worldwide (Airbnb, n.d.). But here, again, are legality issues. These aren't so important to leisure travellers, but to corporate ones – where employers need to provide duty of care – the picture is somewhat different.

Nonetheless, Airbnb is fighting to win market share in this sector. It's launched a business travellers' website with accommodation options meeting certain standards. And there are times when it makes sense to use Airbnb instead of a hotel, for example, for team meetings or workshops, for longer stays, or when hotels are booked out.

Hotels are now catching up with and are investing in other 'sharing economy' accommodation platforms. For example, Hyatt invested in Onefinestay, a British start-up renting out prestige homes in London, Paris, New York and Los Angeles (Skift, 2015). It's a sector to watch – especially in cities where demand is high and supply is low.

Dining and Entertainment

It might surprise you, but this is a category in its own right. If you've got a lot of a little, you'll eventually have a lot. And that's how it is with dining: one dinner isn't a lot, but multiply that by 1,000 travellers a day and the costs begin to have an impact on the travel budget. For a long time, dining and entertainment costs were classified as 'hidden spend', because it's been difficult to find out how much is being spent.

However, today, thanks to mobile and technology advances, some companies have dining programmes, like Dinova, in place. They provide a network of restaurants where travellers can get discounts – without coupons or vouchers, simply by paying with a corporate credit card. On its website, Dinova states that corporations and small businesses spend over $50 billion each year in restaurants and on catering (Dinova, 2015) – you see that 'little' is becoming very large indeed.

Mobile Phones

Just a quick word on mobiles, which generally don't fall into the realm of the travel managers' budgets. Note though, that travellers generate high mobile bills, and it's a good idea for travel managers to get together with procurement (or whoever else is making the mobile deals for the company) and check that the best roaming charges are negotiated. It might also be an option to use 'add-on' services for the duration of a trip; that is, buying a certain amount of minutes and mobile data for a specific location.

Travel managers should also provide tips on using mobiles abroad through their travel programme updates and communication. This might be something like 'use Wi-Fi where available', and 'turn off background updates for Facebook' (and all other non-company related apps).

Other Travel Stakeholders

Aside from the travel managers, the travel management companies and all the suppliers above, there are some other providers that have a part to play in this labyrinth of services: the global distribution systems, the consultants, the associations and organisations and (who'd have thought) the travellers themselves. Let's round this chapter off by looking at these in turn.

Technology Providers

There are many companies today providing technology services to the travel industry, and, as was said before, this is only going to continue. The most important to know are the GDSs, but there are others who provide services to the 'coming-home' side of the trip: expense management tools, and those suppliers trying to crack the 'end-to-end' solution.

GDS – Global Distribution System

Generally known in the industry by the abbreviation GDS, the global distribution systems have been the foundation of the travel industry for a long time. They provide a platform to find out about flight schedules, as well as availability and prices of airlines, hotels and car rentals. This is done by linking the supplier's individual computer reservation systems (CRS) into the GDS. And this is what travel agents use to book. Sabre and Amadeus are the largest providers, followed by Galileo and Worldspan (both owned by Travelport).

Sounds rather outdated doesn't it? But it's true. Most of flight bookings are still made through this data architecture of the 1960s. But technology has advanced, and the GDS providers are working on improving their services to meet a new kind of demand. Travellers want to be able to compare services 'like-for-like', but at the moment it's very difficult. While base prices can be compared, additional options, like luggage or amenities, are generally not included or even portrayed. Besides these differ from airline to airline.

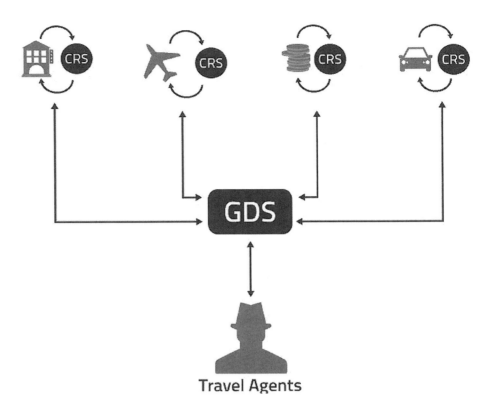

Figure 4 - The GDS

In a world in which suppliers are fighting to get direct bookings, it's the GDSs that we must place our hopes on to come up with a novel way of visualising, comparing and booking travel services. The NDC, discussed in the last chapter, might be just the ticket – or something else will come along.

Expense Solutions

Companies like Concur are at the forefront of offering expense solutions that neatly tie in with the overall travel experience. In chapter five there's more about expenses and how this ties into the trip experience, but it's good to know here that these stakeholders exist.

While today they're exploring more services and, as mentioned, the 'end-to-end' solution, let's focus here on the core business of expense management. Concur offers a mobile-based solution allowing travellers to take pictures of receipts on the road that are uploaded to the expense report. No manual filing is necessary, making this a godsend for travellers (Concur, 2015).

Consultants

Every industry has its own consultants. And there are companies who have made consulting their core service, like PricewaterhouseCoopers (PwC) and Deloitte. They provide clients with support, either on specific projects or on an ongoing basis. They are the experts; the people to turn to in times of need, when employees can't see the wood for the trees. When looking at this from the outside, it often seems a bit bizarre that an external firm needs to provide help to, for example, process optimisation. But in reality, politics and company culture are often so engrained that it needs this external support to bring change!

The same applies for the travel industry. Consultants are needed to look at and advise on (for example):

- Travel policy and strategy
- Supplier negotiations
- Traveller behaviour
- Stakeholder communication
- Business intelligence and analytics
- Outsourcing

So let's take a look at some travel consultants who work specifically in corporate travel. Each of the big TMCs have its own 'independent' consultancy, and it's these we're going to focus on.

Global Business Consulting by American Express' Global Business Travel offers help for most of the above; however, it doesn't mention traveller behaviour specifically. The key message on its website is: *"Whether you're looking for a little help on a specific issue or a total travel management solution, Global Business Consulting can provide the services you need"* (Global Business Consulting, 2015).

CWT also offers consulting services through its Solutions Group. Business travel has its own dedicated webpage and the key phrase here is: *"Tailored solutions for strategy, sourcing, distribution and ongoing optimization"* (CWT Solutions Group, 2015). The following graphic shows an overview of its services (CWT Solutions Group, 2013).

The third one to mention is Advito – the independent consulting arm of BCD Travel. In contrast to the other two, Advito doesn't offer a key message on its website. Instead, key publications are promoted, like the Industry Forecast 2016, white papers and the blog. There are pages dedicated to what Advito can do, of course, but the homepage is all about opening up communication and engagement (Advito, 2015).

There are many more companies consulting on business travel (amongst other things), and there are a lot of independent consultants as well. These are people who have worked for a long time in the industry and feel they can now add more value in the capacity of consultant.

Now that you know what corporate travel consultants do, and have an inkling of the main players in the field and their services, you might ask yourself the question 'what value do they add?' In part, the answer goes back to the beginning of this section. A look from the outside is often helpful to see barriers or inefficiencies that are hidden to those working inside.

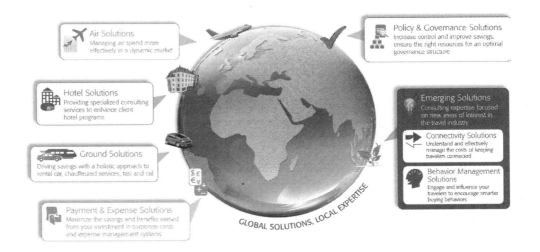

Air Solutions
Managing air spend more effectively in a dynamic market

Hotel Solutions
Providing specialized consulting services to enhance client hotel programs

Ground Solutions
Driving savings with a holistic approach to rental car, chauffeured services, taxi and rail

Payment & Expense Solutions
Maximize the savings and benefits earned from your investment in corporate cards and expense management systems

Policy & Governance Solutions
Increase control and improve savings, ensure the right resources for an optimal governance structure

Emerging Solutions
Consulting expertise focused on new areas of interest in the travel industry

Connectivity Solutions
Understand and effectively manage the costs of keeping travelers connected

Behavior Management Solutions
Engage and influence your travelers to encourage smarter buying behaviors

GLOBAL SOLUTIONS, LOCAL EXPERTISE

Figure 5 - CWT's Business Travel Consulting

The other part is focusing on the problem without playing the blame game or looking for internal company reasons to solve it. This is about innovation; looking at the problem in a new way and thinking outside the box to solve it.

However, working with consultants means companies need to know what they want. And it's not unheard of that they only find out what they want by going through the process and rejecting the results, simply because when they started the consulting process their own goals weren't clear to them. As a result, you often find companies hiring a second consultant who then gets all the credit.

Consultants are also engaged with producing white papers and case studies. They're known to speak at events and share knowledge and so–called 'best practices' – to promote their services, but also to develop the industry further and showcase new opportunities.

Advito's Industry Forecast is a highly regarded publication. The annual report (and quarterly updates) look into current and possible future travel developments, including price forecasts for air and hotels across the regions.

Associations

There are several local, regional and global associations in the corporate travel world. They serve the industry as platforms to share knowledge, education and ideas to further development. You could say they take some of the consultant topics and make them available to a broader audience. But before judging them for this, consider a product lifecycle and its adoption as showcased in the image below (Abouzeid, 2011).

It starts with an idea and a couple of interested parties, so-called 'innovators'. But it takes time and true value for the product (or service) to reach the masses. And that's what the associations do: test ideas, get a conversation going, assess their value and, later, educate the industry on those products and services that made it through.

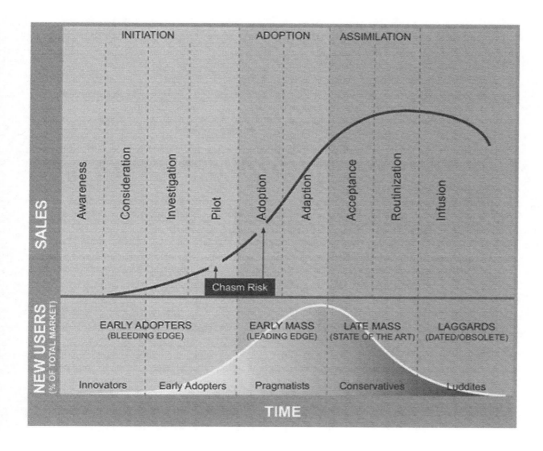

Figure 6 - Product Lifecycle and Adoption

113

Associations work with travel managers, TMCs and travel suppliers (including all those mentioned in this chapter) to bring the industry together and benefit from experience. They also facilitate networking and relation-building. Throughout the year they put on small- and large-scale events for people to come together.

Associations also offer research opportunities that are generally sponsored by one or more corporation. Their own membership base and interconnectedness means research is often more sound than if a corporation tried it on its own.

Lastly, it's the associations who use their lobbying power to make sure the industry has a voice in the local, regional and global economy and with governments.

ITM - Institute of Travel and Meetings

The ITM is the UK's corporate travel association, it partners with GBTA Europe – and, thus, the global GBTA as well.

> 'Members join the association to increase their knowledge and expand their contacts network, combining these to improve their company's business travel programme and their own career development opportunities at the same time' (ITM, 2007).

According to its website, it has about 2,800 members across the UK and Ireland. Its work spreads over five core areas: knowledge, education and career development, resources and guides, events, member directory and exchange and lobbying.

GBTA – Global Business Travel Association

GBTA is the world's largest travel association. With more than 7,000 members and a reach of 28,000 travel professionals globally, they are a power to be reckoned with (GBTA, 2015). The following page shows part of an infographic outlining their membership benefits.

One of the most-often asked questions in the industry (especially in June each year) has to be 'am I going to see you at GBTA?' In July the global event takes place in a US city. While there's also a European conference organised by the GBTA, also termed 'global', this still hasn't created as much pull as the American one. Possibly because of their speaker line-up, which included Presidents Bush and Clinton in 2012, and many other high-profile figures since.

But to be fair, its focus isn't exclusively on the global stage. Part of what makes GBTA attractive, particularly in North America, is its chapters. Cities have their own local GBTA initiative where they can share ideas more frequently and get together for lunch or coffee.

Aside from the local chapters, GBTA also has working groups in place for specific industry topics like Corporate Social Responsibility and Travel Risk Management, to name but a few. These are managed by industry volunteers coming together to share ideas and thoughts – and also to listen and learn.

GBTA At A Glance

GLOBAL MEMBERS

6000+

The largest and most extensive business travel network in the world.

289.8 BILLION DOLLARS

According to GBTA BTI™, U.S. Business Travel is expected to rise in 2014 to $289.8 billion dollars, which is an upgrade from the $272 billion last year.

$$$

Global Reach

GBTA Members are located across the world: North America, Africa, Asia Pacific, Europe, Latin America.

Convention

The Business Travel Event of the Year®

6000+ Over 6,000 business travel buyers and industry suppliers share knowledge, exchange ideas, and connect.

400+ Over 400 suppliers on the expo floor are excited and ready to show how they can help you, or your company, achieve its goals.

EDUCATION

GBTA ACADEMY — The GBTA Academy is designed to power the careers of business travel professionals using education to fuel recognition and advancement.

WEBINARS — Web-based distance educational programs that allow GBTA members and non-members to participate in live interactive programs on business travel industry topics and issues.

Online Training — Online Training provides skill-building opportunities taught by experienced industry professionals.

CAREER ADVANCEMENT

GBTA CAREER CENTER:

Gain access to a highly qualified database of the latest job postings in the business travel industry.

Global Leadership Program (GLP)

Manager-Level Program

Fundamentals of Business Travel Management

GBTA ACADEMY

Executive-level business education providing a broad overview of leadership, finance, marketing, and management.

Provides advanced expertise in developing and managing a travel program.

Curriculum covering the full range of the basics of business travel management - safety, policy, trends, performance, and more.

Figure 7 - GBTA At A Glance

Another core part of GBTA's work is its research focus. Through various sponsorship agreements, corporate travel suppliers have the chance to lead innovation and get recognition for developing the industry. Often, findings from these studies are presented at the conferences and spark a lot of interest, questions and topics for discussion around the banquet tables.

ACTE – Association of Corporate Travel Executives

Lastly, let's have a look at ACTE. On its website it describes itself as such:

> *'The Association of Corporate Travel Executives (ACTE) has a 25-year reputation for leading the way corporate travel is conducted. As a global association, comprised of executive-level members in more than 100 countries, ACTE pioneers educational and technological advances that make business travel productive, cost-effective and straightforward. ACTE advocacy and initiatives continue to support impactful changes in, safety and security, privacy, duty of care and compliance along with traveler productivity that supports global commerce'*

(ACTE, n.d.).

Figure 8 - ACTE: Working Together

Figure 8 showcases its main priorities and how it's helping the corporate travel industry.

Like GBTA, ACTE stages multiple events throughout the year. One of its flagship events in the UK is a roundtable discussion in partnership with the magazine *Buying Business Travel* (BBT). This happens twice a year in London and participants sit around a hollow square table set-up – including the panellists. Some initial questions are asked by the moderator before the general audience takes over questioning the panel or giving opinions. Heated debates have been known to happen, and frequently participants say 'off the record' to indicate to visiting journalists that their opinion best not be published.

ACTE is particularly active with their global education offering. It looks after everyone, whether they're newly joined or industry veterans. It's also well represented in Asia where corporate travel management has developed differently to Europe and North America.

Its 'Around the World' programme is renowned for providing experience and education to travel professionals and students. It's a certified training for global business travel management and is available in different locations throughout the year (ACTE, n.d.

Travellers

Finally, travellers! Possibly the most important stakeholders, because without them we wouldn't need all this fuss, though we often don't consider them in all this hassle neither.

However, that's possibly about to change. As of the past year or two, voices are getting louder about traveller happiness, or rather, the stress they're enduring while travelling and doing business. There's also more talk of engaging travellers in the policy discussion and increasing a sense of ownership.

While travellers aren't considered an active stakeholder in the setting up of corporate travel programmes and policies, their needs are very much taken into account. However, you might quite rightly question this approach of arranging things (and a lot of them) without knowing what's actually needed.

The corporate travel industry still often has the mass-market approach: catering to the majority and trying to find ad hoc solutions for those who don't fit this category. Or ignoring them. But in the consumer world a big shift has taken place away from 'one size fits all' towards personalisation.

The analysis offered by Concur and YouGov (see Figure 9) presents a picture of over 1,000 travellers surveyed in 2012 in the UK (Concur, 2012). As mentioned before, use common sense when looking at figures like this (as they say, 'don't trust any statistic you haven't tweaked yourself'). For example, there's no way of knowing if it's the actual travelling that makes people unhappy in their jobs or if there is something else wrong. Still, it presents some insights into the daily challenges of corporate travellers.

So the next big challenge in corporate travel is including the travellers that we're trying to serve, to better understand their needs, wants and expectations.

Figure 9 - Concur's Traveller Survey Results

Summary

In this chapter we looked at the various stakeholders participating in managing corporate travel. We then discussed the travel manager, the travel management companies, some of the travel suppliers and other stakeholders who play a role in bringing the industry forward.

The travel managers are responsible for a vast range of tasks, from creating a travel programme, writing policy, dealing with day-to-day operations and negotiating annual deals with suppliers to keeping their duty–of–care commitments towards employees on the road.

Working in close collaboration with the travel manager are the TMCs. Their role is developing and they're trying to find their feet in a changing environment. Their role has evolved from traditional booking facilitation to a business model focusing on services like travel risk management and business analytics.

The travel suppliers, airlines, hotels, car rental companies and many others are all trying to gain market share. Partly by negotiating with the corporates and partly through the TMC. They're working hard on differentiating their service offering and bringing a personalised product to corporate travellers.

Other stakeholders include those providing technology, insights, education and information, and those who actually do the travelling. All of them play their part in advancing the industry as a whole.

Now you know some more about the stakeholders, let's delve into the travel programme and see how all these different parties act together to bring a seamless service to the corporate traveller.

Bibliography

Abouzeid, M. (2011, November 28). *Technology Adoption Lifecycle.* Retrieved September 16, 2015, from markabouzeid.wordpress.com/2011/11/28/technology-adoption-lifecycle-revisited/

ACRISS. (2015). *Who is ACRISS.* Retrieved August 25, 2015, from www.acriss.org/who-is-acriss.asp

ACTE. (n.d.). *ACTE Global.* Retrieved January 26, 2016, from ACTE Global: Around the World: www.acte.org/solutions/atw.htm#page=page-1

ACTE. (n.d.). *ACTE Global: Association of Corporate Travel Executives* . Retrieved September 17, 2015, from www.acte.org/about.htm

Advito. (2015). *Advito.* Retrieved September 16, 2015, from www.advito.com/

Airbnb. (n.d.). *Airbnb About Us.* Retrieved September 8, 2015, from www.airbnb.co.uk/about/about-us

American Express Global Business Travel. (2015). *Amex Global Business Travel.* Retrieved August 22, 2015, from www.amexglobalbusinesstravel.com/total-program-management/

BCD Travel. (2015). *BCD Travel - Travel Management.* Retrieved August 22, 2015, from www.bcdtravel.com/travel-services/travel-management/

BCD Travel. (2015). *BCD Travel Facts and Figures.* Retrieved August 22, 2015, from www.bcdtravel.com/get-to-know-us/facts-and-figures/

BCD Travel. (2015). *Business travel management from BCD Travel.* Retrieved August 22, 2015, from www.bcdtravel.com/travel-services/travel-management/

BCD Travel. (2013). *Hidden Spend Infographic.* Retrieved August 22, 2015, from 1ufrwr1faezp-30wik71qj4iz.wpengine.netdna-cdn.com/wp-content/uploads/2014/04/Hidden_Spend_Infographic.pdf

Boehmer, J. (2014, April 15). *Business Travel News.* Retrieved August 21, 2015, from www.businesstravelnews.com/Business-Travel-Research/BTN-s-2014-Small---Medium-Enterprise-Report/?a=btn

Boehmer, J. (2015, August 19). *Business Travel News.* Retrieved August 21, 2015, from www.businesstravelnews.com/Strategic-Sourcing/Pooled-Procurement--Nonprofit-Travel-Buyers-Band-Together-To-Score-Collective-Travel-Deals/?a=proc

BTN. (2015). *Business Travel News Handbook Glossary.* Retrieved August 22, 2015, from www.businesstravelnews.com/Handbook/Handbook.Terms.ashx?HL=tmc

Business Insider. (2015, April 18). *Here's everywhere Uber is banned around the world.* Retrieved September 08, 2015, from www.airbnb.co.uk/about/about-us

Carlson Wagonlit Travel. (2015). *Business Travel.* Retrieved August 22, 2015, from www.carlsonwagonlit.com/en/global/business-travel/

Carlson Wagonlit Travel. (2015). *CWT At a Glance.* Retrieved August 22, 2015, from www.carlsonwagonlit.com/en/global/our_company/cwt_at_a_glance/

Concur . (2012). *Concur Infographic YouGov UK 2012* . Retrieved September 18, 2015, from assets.concur.com/infographic/uk-yougov-2012-business-travel-survey-infographic.pdf

Concur. (2015). *Expense Management Made Easy.* Retrieved September 18, 2015, from www.concur.co.uk/expense-management?icid=en_uk_home_expense

CWT Solutions Group. (2015). *Business Travel Consulting.* Retrieved September 16, 2015, from www.cwt-solutions-group.com/cwtsg/business-travel-consulting/

CWT Solutions Group. (2013). *CWT Solutions Group Infographic.* Retrieved September 16, 2015, from www.carlsonwagonlit.com/export/sites/cwt/sg-gallery/cwt-solutions-group-infographic.pdf

DEHOGA Bundesverband. (n.d.). *Dehoga Bundesveband.* Retrieved January 26, 2016, from www.dehoga-bundesverband.de/

Dinova. (2015). *Dinova.* Retrieved September 08, 2015, from www.dinova.com

Europcar. (2014). *Europcar - Corporate Profile*. Retrieved August 24, 2015, from www.europcar-group.com/en/group/corporate-profile/

Evolve Recruitment. (2015, July 21). *Reed*. Retrieved August 21, 2015, from www.reed.co.uk/jobs/corporate-travel-manager/27598029#/jobs/travel-manager

Forbes. (2015). *The World's Biggest Public Companies - Airlines*. Retrieved August 23, 2015, from www.forbes.com/global2000/list/#header:revenue_sortreverse:true_industry:Airline

FORE. (2015). *About FORE*. Retrieved August 24, 2015, from orgtravel.org/blog/

GBTA. (2015). *About GBTA*. Retrieved September 17, 2015, from www.gbta.org/about/Pages/Default.aspx

Global Business Consulting. (2015). *Global Business Consulting | American Express Global Business Travel*. Retrieved September 16, 2015, from www.amexglobalbusinesstravel.com/uk/corporate-travel-consulting/

IATA. (2015, June 03). *How regulation must keep up with the pace of drone development*. Retrieved August 23, 2015, from airlines.iata.org/analysis/how-regulation-must-keep-up-with-the-pace-of-drone-development

IBM. (2015). *Financial Highlights*. Retrieved August 21, 2015, from www.ibm.com/annualreport/2014/financial-highlights.html

IHG. (2015). *IHG Company Overview*. Retrieved August 23, 2015, from www.ihgplc.com/index.asp?pageid=114

ITM. (2007). *What we do - Institute of Travel and Meetings*. Retrieved September 16, 2015, from www.itm.org.uk/go/site/what_we_do/

Management Solutions UK Ltd. (2015). *Independent Business Travel Consultancy*. Retrieved August 22, 2015, from ms-uk.com/

Newcombe, T. (2015, August 19). *Buying Business Travel - Aer Lingus joins IAG*. Retrieved August 23, 2015, from buyingbusinesstravel.com/news/1924587-aer-lingus-joins-iag-after-shareholders-accept-deal

O'Connel, J. F., & Willams, G. (2005). Passengers' perceptions of low cost airlines and full service carriers: A case study involving Ryanair, Aer Lingus, Air Asia and Malaysia Airlines. *Journal of Air Transport Management , 11* (4), 259-272.

PR Newswire. (2015, February 18). *PR Newswire*. Retrieved September 08, 2015, from www.prnewswire.com/news-releases/the-global-car-rental-industry-trends-forecasts-and-opportunity-analysis-2014-2019---enterprise-rent-a-car--hertz-lead-the-81-billion-market-300037693.html

Skift. (2015, July 21). *It's Beginning: Onefinestay Pilot With Hyatt Highlights Sharing Economy Collaboration To Come*. Retrieved September 08, 2015, from skift.com/2015/07/21/its-beginning-onefinestay-pilot-with-hyatt-highlights-sharing-economy-collaboration-to-come/

STR Global. (2015). *STR Global - A Guide to Our Terminology*. Retrieved August 23, 2015, from www.strglobal.com/resources/glossary/en-gb

The Intrepid Traveler. (2013). *Travel Industry Dictionary*. Retrieved August 21, 2015, from www.travel-industry-dictionary.com/corporate-travel-manager.html

West, E. (2015, October 06). *BTN*. Retrieved January 25, 2016, from www.businesstravelnews.com/Business-Travel-Research/BTN-s-2015-Corporate-Travel-100

Wikipedia. (2015, July 13). *Legacy Carrier - Wikipedia*. Retrieved August 23, 2015, from en.wikipedia.org/wiki/Legacy_carrier.

CHAPTER 4
The Travel Programme

By the end of this chapter you'll be able to:

✓ Have insight into a managed travel programme.

✓ Know about travel policy, how it's created, monitored and adjusted.

✓ Develop an understanding of the operations, both big-picture and detailed, that the travel manager deals with on a daily basis.

Quick Facts

- Travel policy sets out rules and regulations by which employees must comply when on the road. This isn't only important for their safety, but also to make negotiations work.

- Creating policy with input from many stakeholders helps to create ownership within the company.

- Sourcing suppliers and negotiating prices is much more complex in travel than it is for other categories, such as stationary. Mostly because travel managers cannot guarantee the scope of the order.

- Operations in travel management range from demand and behaviour management to corporate social responsibility (CSR) and depend on whether a programme is managed locally, regionally or globally.

- On a normal day, a travel manager might deal with a volcano eruption, reporting tools and supplier visits. Never a dull moment.

Introduction

In this chapter the focus shifts to actually **managing** corporate travel by looking at the travel programme itself. The beginning of the book clarified the distinction between business and corporate travel, and this is where we focus on travel policy, sourcing and operations. The previous discussion about stakeholders helps you find your way through the travel programme as you encounter all those parties again.

First up is travel policy: what is it? Why do companies need it? Does it still have a place in an increasingly digital world? Those are some of the questions we're going to answer. But we'll also look into the many benefits of policy and how to increase traveller (or rather employee) buy-in and ownership.

Up next is a more detailed look at sourcing. You now know the stakeholders, and this section explores the suppliers of travel services in more detail. We explain the importance of sourcing and negotiations and the practicalities of RFPs. We then take it one step further to explore differences in air and hotel sourcing.

Finally, we circle back to the travel manager's other tasks by taking an in-depth look at operations in corporate travel. This covers everything from the nitty-gritty of the day to the overarching framework: bookings, disruptions, communications, demand and behaviour, technology, payments and corporate social responsibility (CSR). It's one part of a dual-core operation; the second being the trip cycle, which we'll explore in the last chapter.

Travel Policy

Travel policy is the backbone of a successful travel programme. It sets guidelines and helps manage travel costs. Several studies suggest that travel spend is the second largest controllable spend within companies after salaries (Mastercard 2012)! And by implementing travel policy, companies could save between 10–15% of travel spend (Egencia 2015) – provided their travellers are compliant, of course.

Depending on the company and its culture, travel policy could be one page long or cover 100 pages. It's everything the traveller may (or may not) do while planning, booking and travelling. So let's take a closer look at travel policy, what it actually is, how it is created and managed, its benefits and also its shortcomings. With that in mind we try to determine whether travel policy is needed – or might possibly be out of date.

What is Travel Policy?

A travel policy sets out the rules and guidelines employees should follow when planning, booking, travelling and expending travel-related costs.

Travel policy can be rules or guidelines – and sometimes a bit of both. The reason for this lies in the approach to managing travel that varies between companies. We've already stated above that the length of the travel policy is dependent on company culture – but that's not the only thing. Company culture has far more impact on travel management than is often realised. In this case, it determines whether a company goes for a mandated, strict approach and rules, or just sets out guidelines to know where travellers are in case of an emergency.

Traditional companies with hierarchical structures often have a mandated approach to managing corporate travel. Start-ups and tech-companies are often empowering their employees to make their own arrangements and then loop the company back in. It goes without saying that these are the extremes on a sliding scale and it's often not as black and white as written here.

An example for an 'in-between' policy could be mandated rules for top frequented routes and a flexible approach to destinations that are off the company's radar. The reasons partly lie in setting up deals with preferred suppliers – which only becomes worthwhile when the company can commit to a certain market share.

Travel Policy Components

Before discussing the various components of the travel policy, let's go back to corporate culture. We often tend to work in isolation, or with some stakeholders who share our ideas. This is not limited to travel management, but is a much broader (and very human) trait. When sitting down and collecting ideas we want to share, we might think of the target group and adjust what we're writing to their needs.

But company documents often overlook company culture as being an important factor to consider. However, when you do take culture into consideration, you already up your chances of employees buying into the document. For now, just bare it in mind – and remember it whenever you sit down and write your travel policy.

So what else do you need to consider to create a travel policy? Let's have a look at the following graphic (Unger 2015) outlining the key components.

Figure 1 - Travel Policy Components

While these don't necessarily represent a particular order, it's a good idea to think about the **company's vision** (and mission statement) when beginning to write policy. Why? Well, businesses want to grow, innovate, retain market share, educate, manage and the list goes on! And it's important to realise that travel enables companies to do just that, so when linking travel policy back to the company's vision, travel managers will get more buy-in from their stakeholders, be it travelling employees or the head of finance.

Let's have a look at the other components in a little more detail.

Preferred Suppliers

The next part of this chapter is dedicated to sourcing: preferred suppliers, negotiations and relationships. In the policy, the travel manager may reference whether only company-approved (preferred) suppliers may be used. It's a good idea to use this part of the policy to educate travellers about preferred options as they often come with benefits (hotels might include Wi-Fi and breakfast, early check-in/late check-out, on-day cancellations, etc.; airlines might include free booking changes or cancellations, extra luggage allowance, lounge access, etc.).

Service

This is about the level of service the traveller is entitled to. It sets out, for example, the threshold for travelling in economy or business class (often dependent on hours of travel time) or the tier rating for hotel stays. It might also differentiate between levels of service and employee status (the CEO might be entitled to a five-star hotel, whereas the analyst stays in a three-star).

Approval Process

Employees wanting to travel often have to go through some sort of approval process which should be part of the policy. If line manager approval needs to be obtained before the booking, there's a need for at least some automation to ensure time for the person to respond. Some companies favour booking the trip while simultaneously asking for approval – so they don't miss out on reduced air fares. The travel manager might also consider whether the approval process should be different depending on trip purpose.

Behaviour

As mentioned above, lead times are important in travel. The common assumption (which holds true in most mature markets) is 'the earlier you book, the cheaper your fare will be'. In the case of working with preferred suppliers, you might also have blackout dates when negotiated rates aren't available.

Behaviour is about advance booking, type of service level (economy/business, three-star or five-star hotel), using the online booking tool (if available) and when to use taxis or public transportation options.

Cost Control

At the start of this chapter, we mentioned how important travel policy is in controlling travel spend. And while a lot of that has to do with making savings, it's almost as important to know how much is being spent! The travel policy helps with budgeting by setting the rules of which travel-related costs are expensed (reimbursed) by the company, and which ones are not.

Stakeholders

Stakeholders are not necessarily part of the travel policy in the sense that there are rules for them to adhere to, but they are integral to the creation, monitoring, managing and communicating of the travel policy. They may be from procurement, finance, human resources, IT, security, sales, facilities, or any other departments that are impacted by travel (either by travelling themselves or by playing a part in the back-office). We come back to the stakeholders and their involvement when looking at creating a travel policy.

Geo(graphical) Scope

By now you've realised that there's more to travel management than meets the eye. For a travel programme, it's important to know the geographical scope the travel manager is responsible for. In small and medium-sized companies, that might mean he's responsible for all travel. In big companies, it might mean he's solely responsible for one country, or maybe a region. Note that in the latter case it's likely there's a global travel policy in place and various local ones to accommodate cultural differences (that's country cultures more than company cultures). This is discussed in more detail in the operations section below.

Risk Management

While risk management is often set out in a separate travel risk management policy, it's a good idea to put some bullet points on risk in the overall travel policy as well. This could just be a reminder that country briefings are shared before trips, or could be actual guidance on how to behave in highly frequented destinations.

Note that the risk part depends largely on the company's business; if it's the media, you might send journalists to high-risk destinations to report on developments while other companies are trying to get their travellers back home safe.

If there is no separate travel risk management policy in place, it's a good idea to take this as a starting point to write one. While we all believe nothing bad will ever happen to us, it's a good idea to have an action plan in place if something does.

Meetings

Traditionally, meetings weren't part of the corporate travel programme, but it's something that is changing. ITM – integrating travel and meetings – is becoming more and more popular across the globe. Essentially, it's making use of volumes. Travel managers found out they're often using the same hotels as their counterparts who look after conferences and (big) meetings. For negotiations this is important as you can drive better deals by promising more volume.

However, meetings might still just be referenced in the travel policy in terms of changes to transient travel rules or which internal contact to approach if a traveller wants to host a big meeting.

Creating Travel Policy

Looking at the different components of travel policy, you now have a much better understanding of what's involved in creating one. The first step is to get the various stakeholders involved and find out about their needs. Let's have another look at those stakeholders and what they might want to achieve with travel policy.

Procurement

They are in charge of sourcing all kind of supplies for the company – not only travel. Often they're involved in the travel-sourcing process, but their approach is very much on driving costs down. They'll want to ensure that no luxuries are granted. This might sound exaggerated, but since procurement employees often don't travel themselves, they frequently can't relate to the exhaustion a mid- or long-haul flight brings with it. Hence, they look at the bare minimum needed to ensure employees are able to do their job, but may overlook how good a job it will be.

Finance

Their job is to pay the bills at the end of the day and so have an interest in the budget side of travel spend – and the controls the travel manager is putting in place to ensure budgets are adhered to.

While often in line with procurement, they do tend to listen to arguments regarding traveller well-being and can make the connection between exhausted travellers and lost business. Mostly, because the heads of finance do travel.

Human Resources

They have a very different approach to travel policy and it's twofold. Firstly, they are responsible for the company following duty of care regulations. For the travel policy, this means they want to ensure you have given some thoughts to risk management and traveller safety and security. Secondly, they're also responsible for hiring and employee retention. Since the financial crisis of 2008 and the tightened travel budgets, many companies have found they're losing employees because travellers suffer too much stress on the road (these are mainly the so-called 'road warriors' who often only spend weekends at home). In other words, human resources are advocates for some comforts, traveller satisfaction and productivity on the road.

Security

As the name suggests, the security department is interested in the security of the employees – and the company's data. Its involvement in travel policy is likely to be limited to ensuring these parts are covered. Security wants to ensure that guidance is given to employees on how to behave on the road.

IT (Information Technology)

Similarly to security, the IT department's approach to travel policy is limited to the parts it actually touches upon: data security and, more importantly, booking tools. While a travel manager might have a fancy new app in mind that she wants her travellers to use on the road, IT staff are the people she has to convince that it's a safe option (and doesn't 'steal' company data in the background).

They'll also help with integrating content into online booking tools or connecting different data sources – you'll see you have a lot more to do with IT than you may have thought when you took on the role.

Sales

These are the guys (and girls) who actually do the travelling and it's a good idea to involve them in the travel policy. They might not agree with all the other stakeholders, but if they see the travel manager is making an effort and have their well-being in mind, they will be advocates in ensuring employees are buying into the travel policy. It also creates a sense of ownership, which further strengthens compliance.

These are the various stakeholders, but there's more a travel manager can do to ensure the travel-policy creation gets off to a good start – have a look at historical booking data. Find out what are the most frequented routes and most booked hotels; if there's feedback from employees about past travel experiences, use it to form a picture of what people are currently facing – and how the travel manager can ensure that the policy is not restricting but actually enabling travellers to do their job better. Remember: it's all about growing the business while being economical with available resources.

However, listening to stakeholders and looking at historical booking data is only the beginning of creating travel policy. The next step is mapping out all the components as discussed previously. Another step is writing the first draft trying to incorporate stakeholder feedback as best as possible. Note that there are likely to be opposing views. These points need to be discussed with the opposing parties only, rather than involving everyone. It's imperative to let everyone have their say and then come to an agreement. This might take quite some time and possibly require a neutral umpire. However, it's important to make sure an agreement is reached before sending out the first draft to everyone involved – otherwise the battle might be longer and fiercer as stakeholders take sides.

Once the first draft is completed it is sent out to the stakeholders to ask for feedback. Any issues that may be brought forward should be discussed directly with the person involved. It's essential to have buy-in from this group so they can act as policy advocates in future.

When travel policy is finalised and approved it's also shared with all employees. There are several ways to go about it and it's a good idea to use multiple channels. Communication with travellers is a topic under 'operations' so we look into those channels then.

Monitoring Travel Policy

Once travel policy is implemented, it needs to be monitored in order to drive the best benefits from it. There are different levels of monitoring and this involves different stakeholders: the travel manager, TMC and possibly a consultancy – depending on the magnitude of the changes or new implementation. These are discussed below.

Whichever route (or combination of routes) is selected, it's imperative to remember to collaborate with the travellers and bookers, ensuring their feedback is not only heard, but also acted upon – even if it's only to explain why their idea can't be implemented at this time.

Travel Manager

Daily monitoring, like approval processes or dealing with rogue bookings, are the norm for the travel manager. While this might seem tedious, there's more to this process in the long run; monitoring policy over time gives insights into booking behaviour and traveller preferences. And all of this information is important for supplier negotiations and driving savings.

TMC

To some extent, the travel management company (TMC) supports monitoring policy as well as encouraging the client's employees to be compliant. It's the TMC's agents on the phone when travellers ask for a new trip to be booked and are, therefore, perfectly placed to influence decisions – and remind travellers of booking policy. The TMC might also offer reporting or a dashboard view of how the travel policy is performing on a monthly basis.

Consultancy

In case employees don't take to the travel policy, there's always the option to bring in a third party, i.e. a consultancy. They are often better placed to see why travellers aren't compliant because they come to the policy with fresh eyes. As said before, often we can't see the wood for the trees.

While it's good to have various stakeholders monitoring policy, it's even better to know what they should be looking out for. The industry makes use of key performance indicators (KPIs), which are often similar across companies but can be customised to monitor special deals or behaviour dependent on company culture or trip types.

The most important thing to remember for KPIs is that they should be quantifiable – so you have something at the end of the day to compare with. Have a look at this list of KPI options as published by *Buying Business Travel* (2013):

- Transactions/spend by traffic type (air, hotel, rail, ground transportation) and by origin country
- Average transaction values
- Cost per mile (air)
- Top routes/vendors
- Top travellers
- Fare type by class
- Advance booking ratio/savings
- Achieved/lost opportunity
- Contract performance goals
- Policy compliance
- Trip purpose
- Online booking tool adoption
- Credit card leakage

Some of these haven't been discussed yet, but they're part of this chapter under the sourcing and operations sections. For the moment let's focus on three of these: fare type by class, advance booking and online booking tool adoption. The information obtained is crucial for business intelligence, and that's discussed again further on in chapters four and five.

Fare Type By Class

The policy states the threshold for economy or business class air travel. This is often measured by travel time, for example, flights up to six hours should be booked in economy class (that's why the measurement is often called economy class ratio in the industry).

However, with the emergence (and increasing popularity) of premium economy class it's an idea to include this in the policy as well – though remembering that not all airlines offer this product.

Advance Booking

This is another good KPI that is somewhat easy to measure; how far in advance are employees booking their trips? The policy should outline cut-off dates. These might vary depending on trip distance, for example, a short-haul flight should be booked seven days in advance, while a long-haul flight should be two or three weeks.

Online Booking Tool Adoption

Everything is moving into the digital world and travel is no exception. Especially for 'simple' trips (there and back again) OBTs (online booking tools) are a good option. For trips involving multiple cities calling a travel agent is currently still the preferred way to book. But it's only a matter of time before technology copes with that challenge as well. Policy should spell out when to use what, so that the online channels are used to full potential. After all, they're less costly than arranging travel over the phone.

Monitoring policy is important, because it helps identify traveller behaviour. It's also possible to drive travellers to a certain supplier when the travel manager finds that monthly targets on negotiated rates aren't met. Finally, it allows a deeper understanding of why travellers aren't complying to policy.

The Future of Travel Policies

At the global conference of the Association of Corporate Travel Executives (ACTE) in Paris in November 2015, there was a lot of talk about the future of travel policies, though the title wouldn't have given it away (Improve your life with predictive data 2015). While we're going to look at business intelligence and predictive analytics in chapter five, during the session there was a lot of talk about something different as well: personalisation.

Personalisation and traveller-centricity are buzzwords currently circulating the industry. And they link into travel policy, because the times of mass marketing and mass communication is over – for now (and hopefully for good). It's time for the individual to be recognised for being a person in his or her own right.

This means adjusting travel policy to the needs (and preferences) of individuals. Even though it's unlikely there'll be personal travel policies in the short-term future, it's very likely that employees will be grouped together to allow at least a more customised approach. This could be done, for example, by business department: sales, marketing, research and finance all have different needs mainly because their travel patterns vary considerably.

Another approach to ease into personalisation is making use of the corporate identity of the company. By simply providing branded credit cards or branded travel tips, employees are reminded of the company they work for – and the loyalty they have for it. Just a few logos added into the itinerary or agenda could change compliance rates considerably and pave the way for further customisation.

Sourcing

As you might remember from the introduction of this chapter, we're going to take a closer look at sourcing and the role travel suppliers play in the industry. Firstly sourcing is defined in general terms and then applied to corporate travel. But you also need to know how to source, so we take a look at negotiations and the (im)practicalities of requests for proposals (RFPs). Furthermore, there's differences in sourcing depending on which suppliers you want to integrate, so we distinguish some practices between air and hotel.

What is Sourcing?

Generally, in business, sourcing refers to various procurement processes mainly split between strategic and global sourcing. Since you might find travel management within the procurement department, it's good idea to gain some knowledge of what sourcing means overall before looking at the travel specifics.

People often roll their eyes when talking about procurement as they don't see its value for what it is – or maybe rather what it could be. But more of that after the following discussion on the two aforementioned sourcing processes.

Strategic Sourcing

> *Strategic sourcing is an institutional procurement process that continuously improves and re-evaluates the purchasing activities of a company.*
>
> (Wikipedia 2015)

In other words, strategic sourcing is about buying items for the company – usually those that one has to buy again and again. This central function is all about cost cutting and savings but also about committing to bulk purchases or scope of order. That's the reason you find travel teams often situated within the procurement department.

But for the moment let's ignore travel and focus on general strategic sourcing. As an example, let's take a look at stationery orders, after all, everyone needs paper, pen and envelopes for their work.

In its simplest form, procurement refers to the department responsible for negotiating and buying things for the company at the lowest price possible.

Strategic sourcing is about making smart purchasing decisions for necessary (and often recurring) items. Going with our stationery example, it's safe to say that needs will differ, depending on the size of a company. However, the company should have a good idea of how much stationery they use in a quarter or even annually. If they don't have historic data available on usage, they might use a guesstimate (slightly more accurate than a guess, but not quite as sophisticated as a calculated estimate). Together with the supplier, the procurement team negotiates a deal: a fixed (and discounted) price for stationery in exchange for a commitment of a certain scope of order or an amount.

Usually, there is also a percentage discount available on products the supplier can supply, but that are not needed frequently enough to make it worthwhile to include in the deal. This helps with the relationship and ensures market share as well as increasing customer loyalty.

What's important to remember is that strategic sourcing is about recurrent purchases: knowing what's needed and negotiating to get it at the best price possible.

Global Sourcing

The main difference to strategic sourcing is that global sourcing is about finding opportunities to save or become more efficient by using resources outside of the company.

> Global sourcing is the practice of sourcing from the global market for goods and services across geopolitical boundaries.
>
> (Purchasing & Procurement Center n.d.)

Basically, global sourcing means outsourcing: finding a company or supplier who can provide a service more efficiently and effectively (and cheaply!) than if it was done in-house.

The link to travel management is not quite as obvious as with strategic sourcing, but it's as meaningful. A lot of corporate travel is done to find sourcing options! So thinking in travel terms, you could say that strategic sourcing is the domain of the travel manager, while global sourcing is what travellers do.

Let's look at an example to make sure we're on the same page about understanding global sourcing (and differentiating it from strategic sourcing). The most prominent one is possibly customer service outsourcing. Who hasn't been on the phone to a service centre where the attendant reads a script off the screen and you're often not any wiser than before the call?

Lately, many companies are aligning travel with procurement to make use of the latter's expertise in negotiations and ensure savings are achieved. However, often other parts of the travel programme (like risk management or health) drop off the radar.

Companies have spent time analysing their customers' questions (or so I hope) and found that most of them can be answered quickly by implementing a standard answer that fits 80% of the time (ever heard of the 80/20 rule?).

The benefit for the company is they don't have to spend resources on recurring tasks that take them away from their main business. Often, specialised call centres also develop quality work flows and are able, over time and with training (if provided), to answer questions that don't fall into the standard frame.

But now let's find out how all this relates to travel management and, more importantly, how sourcing is done in this sector.

Sourcing in Corporate Travel

We already saw how strategic sourcing relates to travel management – the necessity to save money, cut costs and buy bulk for better prices is very much replicated in travel sourcing. However, there are some key differences: suppliers might not be able to supply all locations (hotels) or destinations (flights), business needs (and therefore flight patterns) might change depending on the economic situation, expansion, or retraction of the company and demand is generally not evenly spread across a time span.

Furthermore, there's the traveller to consider. What risks might she encounter in a location abroad? How productive will he be in a 9am meeting, after an overnight (so-called 'red-eye' flight)? Or even: is there an alternative to travelling in this case?

Let's take a look at how travel managers traditionally source suppliers by means of RFP (request for proposal), negotiations and, more recently, dynamic pricing.

The Request for Proposal (RFP)

The first hurdle a supplier has to face is being invited to an RFP; that is, being 'allowed' to partake in bidding for a business they might (or might not) win. So how does a supplier make the list? On their side, they can do their homework and check which companies have stayed with them in the past. They naturally know who they have contracts with already so that's a good place to start. But often, especially with hotel bookings, travellers book outside the programme according to their preferences (or loyalty benefits). If a hotel can prove they have a certain amount of travellers from a company staying with them already, it can try to contact the travel manager directly – or go through the TMC.

The Pareto Principle, coined the '80/20 rule', and found that 80% of land was owned by 20% of the population (Reh 2016).

This finding was replicated in many different situations and is today widely used for sales and marketing.

Alternatively, the travel manager invites suppliers to participate. Often this is done using last year's list and researching whether a particular destination might be dropped and/or another one added. The data needed is generally supplied by the TMC and frequently the account manager supports the travel manager in the process of sifting through the various suppliers to choose from.

The RFP itself is a somewhat lengthy document. It outlines the scope of the programme and gives information about the evaluation process. Through the use of appendices and templates, suppliers know what format to use when sending data back to the travel manager. Naturally, it's important that all suppliers use the same standards, so data can be merged and analysed to find the best deals instantly and negotiate where necessary.

Note that RFPs are underlying a strict non–disclosure agreement (NDA), and part of the parcel is an agreement in which both parties (companies and suppliers) agree not to share the data or indeed prices with third parties. If the company wants to involve their TMC or consultancy in the bidding process they also have to sign the NDA.

In 2002 GBTA (which at that time was NBTA = National Business Travel Association) launched a template for airline RFPs. This document still exists (you can search for it online under 'NBTA airline RFP template') and provides travel managers with a road map (Jonas 2002), including information they'll need to gather on:

- Pricing
- Value–add options
- Customer service items
- Management support
- Programme support elements
- Labour issues

The template also details common pitfalls to watch out for.

Note that there's a separate template for hotel RFPs! It's different questions to ask and also different ways of pricing. Not only that, but yield management is nowhere near as advanced with hotels than as it is within the airline industry.

Negotiations and Dynamic Pricing

Once the RFPs are filled in, the travel manager needs to check and compare the prices offered. During this process they look for value for money – not necessarily the cheapest price. In other words, if a four-star hotel charges just $10 more than a three-star, the four-star is already in a better position for selection. On the air side it could be the difference between a traditional carrier and a low-cost airline or whether routing is direct on preferred routes.

The analysis of invited supplier RFPs will soon shed light on who is shortlisted to participate in further negotiation and fine-tuning of agreements. This is traditionally done by email (and/or meetings), but today more often travel managers select an e-auction process for procuring hotels. As they have to select properties in many destinations, they open an internet-based auction process during which all invited suppliers bid for the business with the travel manager trying to bring prices down. It's a time-limited process and often comes with technical challenges (computers freezing, lost internet connection) and the looming possibility (for the hotel) of not being selected.

As mentioned, an alternative to negotiated rates is dynamic pricing. This is already established in airline negotiations, but hotels are just starting to implement it (often to the dismay of travel managers). Dynamic pricing means instead of negotiating prices per hotel, a chain-wide discount is agreed, which is then applied to the best available rate (BAR) on the day. While huge savings are possible in off-peak times, travel managers don't have as much control over budgets as with an up-front negotiated price; dynamic pricing is demand-based. So if Elton John performs in New York, hotels are going to be booked out quite quickly – thus driving BAR rates up for the dates in question. The hotels argue that the corporate traveller still gets the discount, but travel managers fear rates might increase overall.

A big benefit of dynamic pricing is that there are no 'black-out dates' – days that are predetermined by the hotel on which corporate rates cannot be used at all. With that in mind, travel managers are likely to see true value and benefits in this new form of hotel pricing over time.

Travel Policy and Sourcing

Now let's try and loop this back to the beginning of this chapter: travel policy and the effects it has on future negotiations. In the section about strategic sourcing we discussed stationery orders as an example – you commit to a scope of order for a preferable price. In travel it is similar, except that it's difficult to guarantee the scope of order.

On the one hand there's a lot of changes in the world happening all the time. And that might mean a business reason to go to a certain destination ceases to exist. The airline loses business because the rates aren't booked anymore. Note that airlines schedule services by demand and might now fly half-empty aircrafts around because business dropped (this was very much the case after the financial crisis until the airline industry adjusted by grounding planes and flying less frequently to certain locations).

On the other hand, there's the traveller to be considered as well. How do you ensure they book with the supplier you so carefully selected? That's where travel policy comes in.

Booking In Policy

As discussed earlier in this chapter, there are companies with strict and mandated policies. In this case, reimbursement might be stopped if a traveller books outside of policy. It's very much a 'stick' approach, however, and doesn't generally account for traveller preferences or, more importantly, traveller well-being. The plus side of a mandated travel policy is knowing with quite some certainty the scope of order on a particular route or for a certain hotel (for argument's sake, let's assume in this example that there won't be changes in business within the next 12 months). Being able to confidently state the scope of order should result in a better discount (or more perks) negotiated by the travel manager.

So why don't all companies mandate travel policy? There's quite some merit in the 'carrot' approach of incentivising good behaviour rather than shaming the bad. Using campaigns to alert travellers to offers, preferred suppliers and, most importantly, benefits of booking through the company channels can lead to high compliance, too.

Booking Out Of Policy

While being compliant helps the travel manager negotiate good discounts and perks for the future, booking outside the travel policy can have a huge knock-on effect for the whole company. Travel managers can't meet the bookings agreed in the deal and this jeopardises future negotiations.

What's often more frustrating is travellers staying (or flying) with preferred suppliers – but not using the company's booking channel. Thus their reservations aren't captured, aren't eligible for the discounted rate and don't count towards the scope of order. There is some good news though: technology is now able to read booking confirmations and capture all the information for the travel manager (like TripLink from Concur (Concur 2016)). All the traveller has to do is send the confirmation to an email address and the travel manager will have a report. This doesn't solve the problem instantly, but at least leakage is now transparent and steps can be taken, either to avoid the issue in future or to change travel policy and booking channels to a more empowering model.

Sourcing and travel policy are joined at the hip to make the most of both. And you might think that creating, monitoring and updating travel policy, plus annual (or bi-annual) sourcing projects are more than enough for one person to deal with. But that's not all; the travel manager is also (and maybe more so) in charge of the operations of the travel programme.

Operations

The operations of a travel programme are quite different from the general use of the word in other industries. Nonetheless, travel managers do look after the efficient running of processes: bookings, cancellations, amendments, disruption, communications, expenses – the list just goes on and on. And it's their job to make sure everything is going smoothly or, if not, jump in and get things back on track.

This part, therefore, looks first at the differences in operations, with an emphasis on tasks and whether travel programmes are managed globally, regionally or locally. Next is managing the big picture. Similar to travel policy and sourcing, there are other categories a travel manager needs to work in, though they generally overlap or flow into one another. Finally, when you thought you had heard about all the things a travel manager has to do, we take a look at managing the detail – that is, the daily interruptions to the travel programme.

Differences in Operations

Operations are easiest when you have just one traveller – and that is yourself. Once you have to look after someone else it all tends to go pear-shaped, unless you have a strong travel programme in place that provides you with a framework of what to do when. But even when you do, there are bound to be challenges. These could be on a large scale, like legal differences in some countries where your company has offices in or they could also be on a small scale, like differences in interpretation in a local office.

Let's look at this in more detail, starting at the local level. For the moment, let's consider the travel manager is in charge for all operations locally and for a company that's operating in only this country as well. Depending on size of the business and need for travel, they might hire a TMC or use their virtual services by connecting through their online booking tool (OBT) and have support when they need it. The travel manager is in charge of policy, sourcing and operations single-handedly. This means there's no chance of misunderstandings through interpretation but on the flipside it could mean that some items drop off the to-do list (or aren't as carefully considered because of a lack of time).

On the other hand, you might find a local travel manager working as part of a team for a global company. While responsible for the operations of the country, they also must align with the global travel policy and guidance from regional and global travel managers. You can see that might become political or messy. However, on the plus side there's a vast support network and even though there's still plenty to do, generally you are more likely to have the time to do a thorough job.

A level above, you find the regional travel manager. Often 'sitting between chairs' as they try to fulfil global guidance while managing local differences as well. Depending on the region, they may be lucky to work with just one TMC (for example, this might work well for North America), usually though, they're juggling two to three TMC partners in different countries. The below provides some insights on business intelligence – and the difficulties of non-standardised reporting.

Finally, at the top level is the global travel manager, overseeing all operations for all countries the company has offices (or subsidiaries) in. They are mainly charged with writing travel policy loosely enough for local travel managers to adjust while maintaining alignment with company and cost-savings goals. Similar to the regional travel manager, they deal with many TMC partners across the world and are the main contact for the company's travel needs (they're the one in charge for sourcing TMCs, too!).

Before getting into the big picture of operations, let's quickly discuss why it's so difficult to find one TMC to service the whole world for one company. At a glance it looks like all problems would be solved immediately if consolidation was an option – so why isn't it done? Some companies have tried in the past, but have encountered difficulties – mainly with inconsistent service levels within regions or certain countries. To understand these inconsistencies, you need to know that TMCs often partner with regional or local agencies to broaden their scope. These partners fulfil the TMC requests and often serve other masters as well. Hence, even though standards are provided by the TMC to ensure a minimum service level is adhered to, it's often very challenging to enforce and audit this.

Managing the Big Picture

As stated in the introduction, there are a number of items the travel manager has to do, know about, use or apply to the travel programme. These are travel risk management, demand and behaviour management, communications, technology, payments, expense management, business intelligence and CSR (corporate social responsibility). They're all linked to travel policy in some way, either as actual part of it or as method to communicate and negotiate. On the next few pages, let's take a look at all these in turn to understand what they stand for in the travel programme.

Note that this chapter is still about what the travel programme entails – and not what the traveller actually does. The latter is discussed in chapter five.

Travel Risk Management

This topic is essential to every travel programme, and there's far too much to successful travel risk management (TRM) to cover in just a few paragraphs. However, there are some key points that are worth mentioning.

To design TRM policy, the travel manager follows almost the same steps as when writing the travel policy. The difference here is a particular interest in past incidents, that is, what has happened to travellers on the road? This information is the basis for a so-called risk matrix that outlines the likelihood of risks occurring, mapped against the impact this would have on the company – and the traveller. The below is a graphic taken from a white paper on travel risk management (BCD Travel 2015).

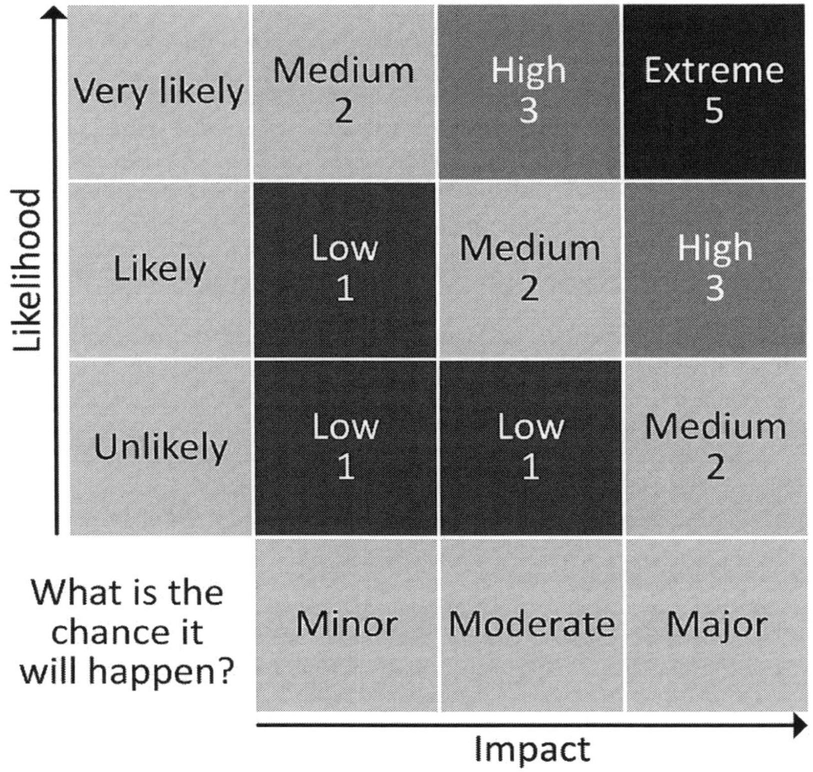

Likelihood	Minor	Moderate	Major
Very likely	Medium 2	High 3	Extreme 5
Likely	Low 1	Medium 2	High 3
Unlikely	Low 1	Low 1	Medium 2
What is the chance it will happen?	Minor	Moderate	Major

Impact

Figure 2 - Risk-mapping

To aid with risk assessment, travel managers usually employ a third-party provider, either through their TMC or standalone. International SOS, Anvil and – new in the market – GEOREACH, are all go-to brands and it can be difficult to decide which is best.

Dependent on the geographical scope of the travel programme, a standard 'off-the-shelf' offering might be just right, but there are many companies in need of a much higher level of support. And this decision shouldn't be taken lightly, as duty of care laws, as well as local and international laws need to be adhered to.

Managing the big picture, in this case, means the TRM provider keeps an eye on the travellers (and those planning to travel in future), and alerts the travel manager of any situations arising that might have an impact and, of course, of any incidents that occur.

We discuss how that might look like in practice and from the traveller's perspective in chapter five.

Demand and Behaviour Management

Before diving into what this means for travel, let's just quickly get the terminology right. Both definitions below have been taken from the white paper *Traveler Management: how to influence your employees to plan, book and travel smarter* (BCD Travel 2013).

Demand management: *influencing the number of trips travellers take.*

For the travel manager to be successful at managing demand they need to be very closely aligned with other stakeholders in the business. After all, the travel manager can rarely decide whether a trip is necessary. Yet it's important that budget holders are aware of costs and keeping an eye on which trips might be combined, or when it's possible to send just one employee.

To achieve demand management, travel managers often place trip authorisation tools into the booking process to ensure employees don't just book anything. This, in turn, is linked with technology (see below) as well as with travel policy – obtaining trip approval is an integral component for companies where this is practiced. This is again more closely looked at in chapter five.

Behaviour management: *influencing the way travellers plan their trips, how much they spend and with whom.*

In turn, behaviour management is easier for travel managers to do – they're the ones who pick the planning and booking tools, as well as carrying out the negotiations with preferred suppliers. But the times of 'one size fits all' are over, as discussed above; marketing to the masses and thinking that an off-the-shelf solution can be applied (and used) by all employees is wishful thinking. Personalisation is coming and we expect to see a lot more of it – especially in the behaviour management sphere.

Why? Simply because people plan their trips differently, they spend their money on different things depending on personal preferences and importance. Many will happily follow travel policy in terms of who they book with, but if they don't know about it, they'll just buy whatever seems best to them.

Currently, travel managers employ gamification as one approach to engage with individual travellers or smaller groups (like departments). They have dashboards of top traveller in policy, or most miles and least spent, or some such to showcase employees what is actually possible and, naturally, makes others want to win, thereby upping compliance levels.

These games are often incentivised, but this depends on the location. There are countries, like Germany for instance, that won't allow this to happen as not all employees can travel (and so can't participate in the game). However, in these locations it's still possible to use gaming, it just can't be connected to (monetary) benefits for the travellers so as not to exclude other employees.

Another way to entice travel policy compliance is the use of behavioural economics. As Dan Ariely's book, *Predictably Irrational* (2009) promises, travellers – just like everyone else – need to be nudged to make logical choices. This can be done by anchoring prices of different travel services so employees develop an understanding of what a reasonable price for a product is.

The travel manager could also use framing for travel options, giving the traveller the feeling they choose 'the right thing' without knowing that their behaviour was actually steered. Another option is decoy pricing, see below picture from the Traveler Management Survival Guide (BCD Travel 2013):

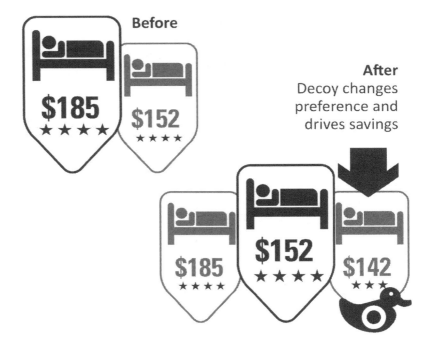

Figure 3 - Decoy Pricing

The possibilities of influencing travellers and reminding them of preferred behaviour are increasing by the day, once again thanks to technology and a deeper understanding of communications. But more of that in chapter five as well.

Communications

We've already touched upon communications and you're quite aware of its significance for the travel programme. Quite simply, if travel policy isn't communicated how do employees know what's allowed and what isn't? Or if the preferred supplier names aren't shared how do travellers know what to book? Yes, you could argue that the employee needs to get hold of the information because it says in her contract to comply to travel policy when on a business trip. But in today's world, who has time for it? And who remembers what's written in their employment contract?

Communications are important to keep employees up to speed with everything their travel management team works on. Naturally, the travel manager doesn't just want to sit on all the information and shame whomever didn't come to enquire about it. But sometimes there's so much to do that communications take a back seat. Or not enough thought is put into the 'how' to communicate information to the best advantage. For example, what use is it if I read the 50-page travel policy during my first week of employment? It might be useful, of course, for the next two weeks, but I'm afraid my memory wouldn't retain the information – nor unearth it at time of planning and booking a trip. So travel managers have to be communication wizards!

There are several methods of communicating: email, intranet, staff magazine or newsletter, a mobile app, or just plain old text messaging. While emails are a great way to share information with loads of people at the same time, they tend to be overlooked, not read or just filed. It's probably a good idea to still use them, even if it's only to 'cover your back' in case someone says they've never heard of that policy before. Another good way of reminding people about the travel programme is featuring bits and pieces in staff magazines or newsletters where attention is brought to one detail – preferably attached to a case study of a real-life employee of the company.

More in vogue today (and here to stay for some time) is text messaging and in-app messaging. This can be triggered based on location to remind travellers what (not) to do. It's very similar to notifications like 'it's now time to check-in' by airlines – only it's provided by your company's travel department. As you will have noticed this is again very much linked to something else: technology.

Technology

It's everywhere. You can't get away from it. In fact, I could've probably linked everything I wrote back to technology in some way. But let's focus on where we are: technology for the travel programme. In some cases, it's enough for the travel manager to be aware of what's happening with technology. That's the trends discussed earlier: hologram meetings don't have to appear in the travel programme – yet.

But there's technology travel managers work with today and have been working with for a long time: the GDS being a prime example. They're part of the travel programme because that's how trips are purchased (at least today, and at least air). However, the GDS is usually part of the TMC offering for the client so doesn't play such an important part in their running of the travel programme.

More important is the online booking tool (OBT) that's also often supplied by the TMC but can be chosen by the company as well. This is the place for trip approval; once an employee books a trip it's rerouted to their line manager for approval. At the same time, technology allows for the rate to be locked in (usually for a certain amount of time). If approval doesn't come quickly enough the price might increase and a new approval process would have to be started. That's why in the past there was a lot of anxiety associated with trip approval. However, thanks to technology, a lot of that is history and employees can quickly plan and book their trips – including obtaining sign-off.

A technology that is making its way into corporate travel management is mobile apps, as stated in the communications section above. Travel managers cannot ignore this much longer and many companies already offer some internal apps that could be made use of. Still, at the moment it's rather expensive technology to create an app that would cater for corporate travel management and so customisable TMC apps are a good alternative.

And there's so much more: door-to-door planning so the traveller knows how much time the entire trip takes and what all the travel options are, gamification: earning points for good behaviour is easily done in an app, virtual collaboration is on the rise once more and could finally have a high impact on corporate travel behaviour. The list is endless and daily there are new innovations – some of which are here to stay, most of which aren't lasting longer than the day they became visible. Lastly, there are also a lot of technological advances in the payment sector, helping both travellers and travel managers to further control cost and make savings.

Payments

To clarify up front, payments in this case are related to sourcing, rather than expenses paid on the road (we come to that in chapter five).

It's one of the back-office functions that needs to be addressed because there's different options for travel managers to choose from and negotiate. Paying suppliers can take many different forms, partly depending on the supplier, partly on the terms and conditions agreed upon.

For instance, looking at airlines, it used to be customary to pay tickets monthly – with a month (or three) delay. The TMC would pay tickets and pass the expense on to the client (plus transaction fee). But like everything else, things are changing and payment terms are tightening up in all industries. New ways of booking, internet-based rather than via the phone, also have an impact on fees charged.

The big problem with many corporate travel payments is that it's done via a central credit-card number that's stored with the TMC. Sadly, a lot of fraud is being reported as the CC numbers get used often and are difficult to keep track off. But there's good news too, virtual cards that are used for one transaction or a predetermined timeframe and a predetermined credit limit are slowly gaining traction in the industry. This makes fraud more difficult and allows travel managers to track transactions on a much more basic level.

Note that the travel manager also needs to address whether employees can be granted corporate credit cards. If yes, he has to do the negotiations with card suppliers, like American Express or, specifically in the area of business travel, AirPlus. If no, he has to make travellers aware they'll have to use their personal credit cards or ask for an allowance before travelling to cover costs.

Expense Management

Payments and expenses go hand in hand. And while claiming expenses is a task the traveller performs post trip (as we discuss in chapter five), there's expense management that needs to be spearheaded by the travel manager.

From their perspective, any solution needs to be compatible with their business intelligence platform. Expenses are a key part to analysing travel spend, controlling costs and keeping on top of negotiated deals. So being able to see data (integrated with other sources) is a must-have for the travel manager.

Business Intelligence

This leads nicely into another 'big picture' topic: business intelligence. Data is not only needed on a day-to-day basis (see below), but also annually for negotiations, for performance reviews, for programme reviews and to know who books out of policy the most.

But getting a true picture of travel spend is a tricky undertaking. While it seems straightforward when first approaching it – after all it's just looking at the transaction data – looking more closely one immediately sees that it's quite a bit more than one bargained for.

Transactions certainly take up a large part of travel spend; mainly the air bookings and quite a few hotel transactions as well. But that's not all that is spent on a trip! There are other things that are consumed and paid for by the company. To get at that data, travel managers must integrate different information streams: booked (pre-trip), transactions (post-trip), credit cards and expense reports.

With this information, they can monitor and adjust their travel policy and drive messaging to meet KPIs, thereby ensuring that supplier contracts are fulfilled on one side and negotiated rates are respected on the other.

Corporate Social Responsibility (CSR)

Lastly, let's take a look at CSR, as many companies are adhering to CSR campaigns and projects. Partly because it makes for a good image and partly because some initiatives are actually legal requirements. It touches upon travel mainly because of CO_2 emissions, standards and savings thereof.

In corporate travel, this subject has always been around; it's been acknowledged in global studies as being important. Yet, until now there hasn't been much action. While it's an important topic, it needs resources (time and money) to do something about it. And that's something travel managers can seldom spare.

But with new regulations and a world that's more and more interested in the ecology of the planet, it might loosen the purse string of some companies to fund initiatives that help travel programmes become greener. And there are already things one can do – take the train instead of a plane for example. Granted, that's easier in Europe than in North America, but people still need to be told about the options available to them (have I ever mentioned communications before?).

One option available to travel managers today is in corporate tools that calculate CO_2 emissions during the planning process. This way the traveller already knows the options and the environmental impact their trip is going to have. Chapter five, yet again, has more information about the tools already available.

CSR audits are becoming more common as well. Companies have to show what they're doing to keep emissions down – even if it's planting trees. And it's not only about emissions. CSR is about community as well, and companies nowadays engage more and more locally. Not only as a provider of employment, but also through sponsoring events or giving to charity.

With that renewed interest in the topic, CSR in the travel programme helps employees cope when they see emissions building up in their profiles. This visual effect is also a good way to get them more engaged and to think about whether that next (plane) trip is really necessary or if virtual means might be enough.

Managing the Detail

A working day in the life of a travel manager isn't often the same as the one before or the one after. There's plenty to do and often the daily challenges take priority over all the other things we've just discussed. It's a common theme in any business: fire-fighting but never really having time or space to prevent fires from starting.

So what are the challenges and opportunities travel managers might be faced with? Let's take a look at some of them, though this isn't an exclusive list, of course.

Booking Enquiries

The classic enquiry that every travel manager I've ever spoken to quotes is an employee wanting to book out of policy for a cheaper price. Sometimes they just do it and are found out later. Sometimes they call in to tell the travel manager that they can book travel much cheaper and basically think they can do the job of the travel manager much better.

Another situation is enquiries from the agency or other members of the travel team about interpretation of travel policy. For example, how much time during a flight stop-over warrants an upgrade to business class or, if that's not possible, when can lounge access be arranged.

And then there's questions about when a negotiated rate isn't available. The travel manager might have to go back to see whether it's due to agreed black-out dates or call the supplier to make sure the correct rates are loaded in the system. On that note, rate audits are always advisable!

Travel Disruptions

Travel disruptions don't always have to be large-scale disasters, they can be something quite insignificant like a two-hour delay that means a connection is missed.

The traveller generally calls the agency to find out what his options are, but travel managers are alerted, too. They need to monitor disruptions as delays can play a large part in the supplier negotiations.

And then there are the big disruptions. Terror attacks, like Paris in November 2015, natural catastrophes, like the volcanic eruption in Iceland in 2010 and health epidemics like ebola in 2014 are happening with far more wide-reaching impact than ever before. Because we live in an era of globalisation, companies often have employees abroad – in all sorts of areas doing all sorts of things. It's paramount for travel managers to know where all the people are and make arrangements when flights are grounded.

Reporting

A lot of the work of the travel manager is about reporting. As we've discussed, historic data and analysis are important for successful negotiations. But on a daily basis? Well, for some of the above, reporting tools come in handy. Otherwise, it's checking how the travel programme is doing: that's looking at the KPIs and, if they're not where they should be, creating campaigns to make sure targets are met.

There's also the supplier reporting the travel manager needs to keep an eye on. Even if the scope of order isn't guaranteed, it should be monitored to ensure numbers are coming close. A well-informed travel manager who knows their figures is always going to be in a much stronger negotiating position.

Lastly, there's the travellers to monitor too. Not only on the rather high-level KPIs, but more basic – which are the routes that are constantly booked out of policy? And who are the offenders? A quick and friendly reminder should always be the first step when talking to travellers about their behaviour, but it might have to be followed-up.

Supplier Visits

On some days, travel managers receive visits from suppliers, either during the negotiation season of course, or just checking in to keep lines of communication open.

Keeping up to date with the reporting is good preparation for these visits, but that's not all. Very valuable for the supplier (and the travel manager at that) is traveller feedback – what works for them, what doesn't and why it doesn't. All this helps the supplier offer a better product, which should help with employee productivity on the road.

Suppliers like airline and hotel representatives are always happy for the chance to talk to the company direct; but the supplier that has the best access is the TMC's account manager. They'll be in touch frequently to discuss the travel programme's performance and what could be done better.

Industry Trends

Finally, the travel manager should take some time out in the day to check the latest news in industry trends. Maybe not every day, but it's good practice to know what's going on. The TMC should be able to point the way with white papers and blogs (or other publications) and there are various media outlets providing coverage for the industry. Many of them have been quoted throughout the book already, like *Business Travel News*, *Buying Business Travel*, *Skift* and *Tnooz* – to name but a few.

All in all, it seems insignificant in comparison with the former part of this chapter, but it's the reality of many a day for the travel manager.

Summary

In this chapter the focus is on the travel programme, its most prominent feature being travel policy. Sourcing is another large and time-consuming process and ties in with policy compliance. However, none of these matter if there aren't operations in place to hold it all together, as we've seen on the last couple of pages.

Travel policy is the guidelines and rules set out by a company to safeguard their employees on the road and to ensure travel is procured at the best prices. It's created by the travel manager and should involve input from various other stakeholders – including travellers – to instil a sense of ownership.

Even with buy-in from employees, travel policy needs to be monitored and changed if needed. A set list of KPIs helps with this process and the account manager is also a good point of call when questions arise.

Sourcing is about negotiating the best deals with preferred suppliers – employee safety and well-being are paramount, though price follows very closely as travel managers are encouraged to save costs wherever possible (and reasonable).

Keeping travellers compliant with policy enhances the scope of order, that is the 'guaranteed' numbers of travellers booking a flight or staying at a hotel. Better deals are possible when travel managers are well-prepared and know their numbers, as well as their travellers' behaviour patterns.

Operations isn't only about the day-to-day processes. A big part of the travel manager's job is about keeping a bird's eye view on the travel programme. Keeping travellers in check, devising campaigns to influence behaviour, gamify CO^2 emission savings and keeping up with all the ongoing developments in the industry give the travel manager plenty to do in the day.

In a way this is all the 'back–office' stuff happening so the traveller can actually, well, travel. And now it's finally time to look at the last piece of the puzzle: the trip cycle.

Bibliography

ACTE. 2015. 'Improve your life with predictive data.' *Global Conference Paris 2015*. Paris, October 15.

Ariely, Dan. 2009. *Predictably Irrational*. Harper Collins.

BCD Travel. 2013. "BCD Travel." *BCD Travel White Papers*. Accessed January 09, 2016. www.bcdtravel.com/resources/knowledge-center/white-papers/.

—. 2015. 'BCD Travel Knowledge Center.' *Travel Risk Management*. February. Accessed January 21, 2016. www.bcdtravel.com/white-paper-download-trm-2015/.

Buying Business Travel. 2013. *Special Report: KPI Dashboards*. April 20. Accessed November 07, 2015. buyingbusinesstravel.com/feature/2020610-special-report-kpi-dashboards.

Concur. 2016. *Concur*. Accessed January 26, 2016. www.concur.co.uk/triplink.

Egencia. 2015. *Egencia*. Accessed January 26, 2016. www.egencia.co.uk/public/uk/en/egencia-solutions/service-solutions/travel-implementation/.

Jonas, David. 2002. *NBTA Aviation Committee Unveils Airline RFP Template*. July 29. Accessed December 26, 2015. www.businesstravelnews.com/More-News/NBTA-Aviation-Committee-Unveils-Airline-RFP-Template/?a=btn.

Mastercard . 2012. *Mastercard Advisors*. January. Accessed January 26, 2016. www.mastercardadvisors.com/_assets/pdf/mca_travel_entertainment_company_travel.pdf.

Purchasing & Procurement Center. n.d. *What is global sourcing?* . Accessed December 12, 2015. www.purchasing-procurement-center.com/what-is-global-sourcing.html.

Reh, John. 2016. *About Management*. Accessed January 26, 2016. management.about.com/cs/generalmanagement/a/Pareto081202.htm.

Wikipedia. 2015. *Strategic sourcing*. September 20. Accessed December 15, 2015. en.wikipedia.org/wiki/Strategic_sourcing.

CHAPTER 5

The Trip Life Cycle

By the end of this chapter you'll be able to:

✓ Know what life cycles are in general, and how this looks for a corporate traveller in particular.

✓ Develop an understanding of the different components of the life cycle, like planning, booking, on the go and follow up.

✓ Understand how the travel programme impacts the traveller and protects their well-being.

Quick Facts

- Life cycles are often used in marketing to determine the phases of a product over time. In corporate travel, the trip life cycle does this too. Crucially, the follow up phase directly feeds into policy and planning to make this a true cycle.

- Planning and booking a trip through corporate channels should be quick, easy and efficient so that as little time as possible is lost searching different options. However, in practice that's not often the case.

- Corporate travellers on the go face different challenges to their leisure counterparts. And what's more, they have to justify their actions and payments to the company.

- Following up on a trip means doing expenses, which can be time consuming, especially if done with hard copy receipts. But it also means that the travel manager can find out how satisfied the traveller was, what worked and what didn't.

- Lastly, and to loop back to the cycle, business intelligence proves the backbone of the industry. With the information collected from travellers and through different data sources, travel programmes become better and more user friendly over time.

Introduction

Finally, it's time to talk about the traveller! But before you get too excited, let's be sure from the start that it still has a lot to do with the travel manager, suppliers, technology and all the other good things discussed in previous chapters. Only now we're considering the role of the traveller within corporate travel management and looking at it from her side of the story.

The trip life cycle, that is the moment from planning a trip until returning and filing expenses, is the last part of this introduction to travel management. And so this chapter starts with looking at different life cycles in general.

An overview of the trip life cycle for corporate travel in particular gives insights into interaction between traveller and travel managers. This is illustrated with a graphic highlighting the different stages –planning and booking, on the go, and follow-up rounding off this subchapter.

Next is a discussion of the main pillars of the trip life cycle, starting with planning and booking. How do employees plan their trips? Is it different from leisure travellers? Do they use the corporate endorsed tools or do they just go on Google? These questions lead the discussion around planning a trip and subsequently getting approval. Trip authorisation, as previously mentioned, is featuring here again and some forms are explained further.

Travel risk management prior to booking is also discussed. What's the security rating for the trip destination? Might this involve different approval processes? We touched on travel risk management before, but it's such an important (and sadly often overlooked) subject that it needs more stage time.

Once planning, travel risk and trip authorisation are taken care off, it's time to book the trip. Will it be online through the company's booking tool? Or through the call centre? Or maybe just do it on your own? It's a field that is currently changing – hence it's important to know what's going on and what might happen in future.

After that, we look at 'on the go'. How different is travelling for a company to travelling privately? A discussion about communication strategies employed by travel managers to keep travellers engaged follows. This part looks at how to influence travellers on the road and remind them of policy when they need it most. Secondary, there's information travellers might want to know, but it's not important enough for travel managers to push out to them. How can companies ensure travellers have access to it?

This is followed by a discussion about ancillary fees: those things travellers might buy as extras to their travel (luggage allowance, room upgrade, lounge access, to name but a few). How can travel managers ensure they're not buying things that are already included in the price? Lastly, we take a look at other 'ad hoc' purchases travellers might make on a trip and what to look out for in terms of being able to expense these purchases when back in the office.

During a trip anything can happen, so there's another look at travel risk management – not preparing for the trip, but what to do when an incident occurs while travelling (and what companies do to ensure help is in place to draw upon).

At last, the traveller gets back home and back to the office. This subchapter deals with all things happening after the trip, including obtaining feedback from travellers about suppliers and services received on the road. Remember that the information collected plays an important part in future negotiations.

We discuss expense management next. What do travellers have to do to claim expenses? What's a *per diem* again? We look at tools that are currently available and discuss the end-to-end process that is going to become reality in the not-so-distant future.

Lastly, business intelligence and data have been constant companions throughout these chapters – but also for everyone involved in the industry. So it's only fitting that this topic concludes this book. We have a look at how travel managers use on-trip data to make better decisions for the travel programme in the future. There's a discussion on mobile apps and how they are going to add more data streams that will help to reveal total trip spend – the Holy Grail for travel managers.

About Life Cycles

Life cycles are used throughout the (business) world to illustrate the different stages an individual or a product (or service) goes through. We look at them as cycles because the stages are recurring continuously. The four seasons are, in a way, nature's annual life cycle – new growth in spring, bloom in summer, shutting down of the system in autumn and deep slumber in winter.

The point is that all stages depend on one another. None can exist if the others haven't been completed. And that's how it is for travel too, whether it's leisure trips (and there's an example below of a tourist life cycle) or corporate travel management. The key differences are in the introduction of complexities. The trip life cycle in a business to consumer (B2C) environment is naturally less complex than adding in a third dimension via the travel manager.

Life Cycles

In marketing, these are generally connected to the product life cycle and its stages are: introduction, growth, maturity and decline (Brassington and Pettitt 2007). This is subsequently followed by a new product, an upgrade or additional services, and thus the cycle starts again.

On the following pages let's look at life cycles in travel, starting with a leisure example from TripAdvisor (Cook 2014). Walking through the different stages, it becomes apparent that there's only one relationship; that of TripAdvisor to their traveller (i.e. customer).

■ Introduction: The Life Cycle of the Traveller

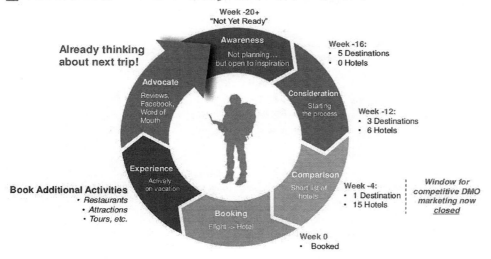

- ◉ TripAdvisor has historically always considered itself as the spoke in the traveller cycle of *Inspiration > Planning > Travel > Review* and repeat
- ◉ However, very *different traveller behaviour and data* can be observed and leveraged at each spoke of the wheel
- ◉ How best then do we not only gather it -- *but take action on it?*

Figure 1 - The Life Cycle of the Traveller

Life Cycle of a Leisure Traveller

TripAdvisor's life cycle has six stages. It starts with awareness, and indeed it's very difficult to be 'unaware' of sunny beaches and faraway places. Advertisements, whether in magazines, billboards or on the television, are an omnipresent reminder of the glamorous world of travel. The point made here is that travellers are aware of the opportunities but haven't connected these with their own holiday plans yet. TripAdvisor claims that the awareness stage is more than 20 weeks before travel booking.

The second stage is consideration. Destinations are looked at more closely. The stage is split with the first half (up to 16 weeks before booking) being devoted to honing in on the destination, without looking at possible accommodation just yet. The second half (about 12 weeks before booking) is down to three destinations and at that point hotels start to become part of the planning process.

While I'm sure it's TripAdvisor's data that has identified these timings, I'm equally certain that travellers aren't conscious of the time elapsing between awareness, consideration and the next stage.

Comparison, the third stage, moves us forward to less than four weeks away from booking. The traveller has settled on one destination (meaning that the opportunity for destination marketing organisations to advertise and convince has ended).

There are up to 15 hotels now in the running and their offers are compared. Note that like-for-like comparisons in travel are very tricky as inclusions often vary by hotel (or indeed supplier) and aren't always transparently shown on websites.

With the comparison and sifting successfully done, it's time to book the trip – hotel and flight. A click and a credit card are all that's needed.

Stage four is about the experience, leaving the time between booking and trip sadly unexplored. In reality, it's more than likely that airline and hotel (and even the booking engine) continue to send offers for the destination, airport parking, insurance and the like. From the traveller's perspective, this is a great time of anticipation of the forthcoming (well-deserved) holiday.

During the experience stage, TripAdvisor reckons travellers book additional activities. Naturally, unless one has booked an all-inclusive offer, meals must be bought abroad. But often there's also interest in going on an excursion, having a spa treatment, visiting a museum or seeing show – something that one doesn't normally do when at home. The purse strings are often looser abroad.

If expectations have been met, the traveller moves to the advocate stage: sharing reviews and pictures on various social media sites and talking to friends and colleagues about their amazing holiday. Word of mouth is still one of the best promotional tools there is – and Facebook (when it's your friends that is) can almost be considered word of mouth, too. Note that expectations might not have been met, and bad reviews might follow, in which case the supplier needs to act quickly to console the traveller and 'save' their rating.

Advocating a destination or a hotel and sharing holiday memories then renews awareness of destinations and places to explore. Thus kicking off the next life cycle of the traveller.

Let's move on to see how this compares to the life cycle of a corporate traveller!

Life Cycle of a Corporate Traveller

As you can imagine, there are many differences between the corporate and the leisure traveller. So let's walk through the different stages again as discussed above and see what happens for the corporate traveller – and when. Afterwards you can see a different graphic of a life cycle bringing the travel manager and traveller into one blueprint.

The awareness stage for the corporate traveller is not based on advertisements or talking to friends about holidays (or at least shouldn't be). For them, awareness starts with a project in the company. This could be working internally on a new product, for example, or a possible sales opportunity.

Consideration of destination is dependent on the travel reason. If it's a client visit, the destination is dictated by the client's office location. But if it's an internal meeting, consideration should be given to finding the best possible location for all participants. That means investigating whether there are offices with space to host a meeting at an airport hub location, what's the most productive way for everyone to meet and where's the cheapest option to meet?

There are tools to calculate this, but there's also common sense: if there are two (or more) participants from one office it might make sense for others to go there.

The next stage for the leisure traveller is comparison of hotels and offers – and, according to TripAdvisor, this takes about four weeks. No such luxury in corporate travel. As we'll see in the next section, planning happens within a day (a couple of hours at most) and comparison is done on the screen, selecting the preferred suppliers that the traveller may have a loyalty account with.

Booking is equally straightforward and done immediately after selection – often using the same online booking tool, although there are other processes the traveller needs to consider in the background, like travel risk management (and preparation) and trip approval.

The experience stage is also considerably different for the corporate traveller. While they, too, must eat and can expense these costs back to the company, their time is much more geared towards business. There's often very little time to indulge in activities such as using the spa facilities of a hotel.

Hence it's difficult to reach a true advocate stage. Corporate travellers might praise hotels they have loyalty accounts with, they will recommend them when everything goes smoothly and they will be frustrated if there are delays to any of their plans. But positive and negative experiences can happen with any supplier, and so it's difficult to get meaningful (and distinguishable) reviews from corporate travellers.

So what about timing? Naturally, this depends on the travel request. If it's a conference attendance, it might be planned up to six months before travel commences. Often it's much shorter notice than that. It could be that planning and booking fall on the same day as travelling, though fortunately that's not too often the case.

The other big difference for corporate travellers is that they aren't completely free in their decisions. They have to follow policy, set out by their travel manager. They are encouraged to be smart when it comes to travel-buying decisions – both before and on-trip.

There's ways to engage with corporate travellers and incentivise good behaviour through gamification (as discussed in chapter four). And, importantly, there needs to be feedback going from the traveller back to the travel manager. This doesn't only help with annual negotiations, but also with informing travel policy. And when travellers see that their suggestions are taken into consideration, they feel a sense of ownership. This, in turn, enhances compliance more than any mandate ever could.

Figure 2 shows the aforementioned graphic: the travel management life cycle. It takes both the traveller and travel manager into account. After studying this graphic, all points are discussed to further your understanding of how these items connect.

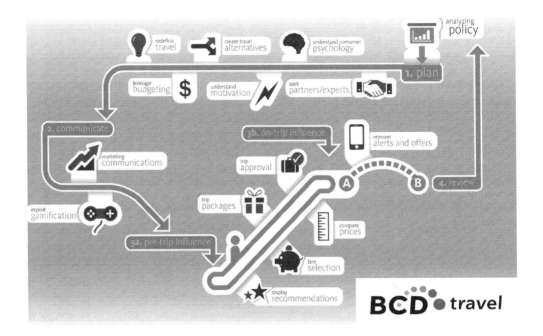

Figure 2 - Traveller Management Blueprint

The Traveller Management Blueprint is taken from a BCD white paper (BCD Travel 2013). Starting the cycle with analysis of the travel policy (this could also be policy creation if none exists so far), it looks first at planning where it's important to understand consumer psychology. In this instance, this means knowing the travellers in order to be able to create or adapt travel policy in a way they are most likely to comply with. Hand in hand with that goes knowing what motivates travellers. This will help later when thinking about incentivising the travel programme.

If the travel manager is new to the industry or has a very diverse traveller spectrum (different ages, locations, educational backgrounds and company positions) to work with, he might want to consider calling in a consultancy to help with the understanding of the travellers and make policy work.

A good way to leverage budgeting is by making sure travellers know the part they play in the overall picture of the company's success – not only through their work, but also through their travel decisions. This strengthens policy ownership and a sense of belonging.

Finally, redefining travel and creating travel alternatives, like virtual collaboration opportunities, also need to feature in the travel policy. Travel managers should make sure policy states clearly that there are 'non–travel' options, what these are and how to access them.

The next stage of the blueprint is about communication. The items discussed above are all very well, but without communicating policy to the traveller (and reinforcing the communication) it might as well never have been written. Using bite–sized information in various different media (as discussed in chapter four) is a good way for employees to keep travel policy in mind.

Gamification is also a good way to engage travellers. Whether this is done 'theoretically' (i.e. on paper) without monetary incentive depends on legal circumstances in each country. Care needs to be taken to check this before communicating any incentives, of course!

Influencing corporate travellers is the next stage, and it's split between before and on–trip.

Pre-trip comes with all the things already discussed in the previous chapter, like trip approval, trip packaging, displaying recommendations, fare selection and comparing prices. It's about using behavioural economics to drive traveller decision into preferred channels.

On-trip is about mobile alerts. This could be through an app or through text–based messaging. As mentioned earlier, notifications could be triggered by time or location. Technology is ever advancing so more options will likely be available soon.

Lastly, the review stage. There are no items mentioned specifically on the infographic, but this is what comes closest to the 'advocate' stage as discussed above. Feedback is integral to travel policy, and, in fact, to the whole travel programme. When travellers are well taken care of, they're also happy employees abroad – thereby having a secondary advocate effect: that of advertising their companies.

Planning and Booking

Now that you have an understanding of the big picture of trip life cycle, it's time to go into a little more detail with all the stages as they are experienced by the traveller. Planning a trip is different from the leisure side, as just discussed, because the reason to travel is business. Planning, therefore, focuses on convenience of options, proximity of hotels to meeting facilities and making the most of the time abroad.

However, there's another side to planning often overlooked for leisure trips: travel risk management. Companies have to comply with duty of care regulations and so travellers should fit some briefing or information (always depending on the destination) into their planning stage.

Another difference for corporate travellers is that they need trip approval from their line manager. Getting trip authorisation depends on the purpose of the trip, the agenda and what it's going to cost. Being prepared with good planning is half the approval done.

Finally, everything is ready for the booking. There are several ways to go about it, often depending on the complexities of the trip. And there are new ways emerging through mobile apps. Whatever way travellers choose, they're sure to have someone they can call 24/7 if something were to go wrong. A luxury few leisure travellers have.

Planning a Trip

Approximately, employees spend two and a half hours researching travel options and over 40% look at more than three sources (Travelport 2010). That's a lot of company time spent on researching something outside of their actual remit. It's a loss of productivity and that, in turn, is a loss of money for the company. And frankly, the researching of best options and best suppliers has already been done by the travel manager.

So where do they look? The same research by Travelport suggests that almost 50% of business travellers start their search on Google. This is followed by visiting airline and hotel websites directly. Note that many corporate travellers have loyalty cards – and because they travel frequently they amass quite a number of miles or points. It's understandable that they want to continue using the same suppliers to collect even better perks. However, there could be legal implications as this is a monetary benefit not available to all employees, so travel managers must be careful to check with their legal departments what the right usage should be.

What are the other ways for corporate travellers to plan their trips? There are several options; traditionally the traveller would ring up the TMC agent and they'd look up all the possibilities on the GDS. An email with the options and travel advice would then be sent out and the employee could select the one best suited to her needs. This is still done for complex itineraries with multiple stop-overs or travel to places that are off the beaten track, where agent knowledge really makes a difference to the traveller – and the booking.

But most companies have invested in technology – online booking tools (OBTs) are now the go-to solution for many employees planning their trips. They're great for 'there-and-back-again' itineraries, but currently still struggle with the more complex requests. Still, it's only a matter of time until tools are able to cope with those itineraries as well.

More recently there have been advances in mobile booking capabilities. While this already exists for individual suppliers through their apps and consolidator apps for leisure travel, so far, there's little possibilities for corporate travellers, at least in terms of booking through their corporate channels.

TMCs are gearing up (successfully) to offer their services and bookings through apps that allow all travel-related necessities to be stored in one place. Offers that are currently booked through the OBT or via the phone can now be sent to the mobile website and are 'translated' to appear in the app's itinerary.

Corporate travellers are generally looking for comfort, convenience and ease of access when they're planning a trip. They'll look for accommodation near the meeting place or the office they're going to visit. If it's a conference they're going to, they'll try to get a delegate rate and stay directly at the venue.

Travel times are also important. Which airport are they using? How much time do they need to plan to get there? For these questions and for better planning capabilities, there have been some tools on the market for some time now. KDS Neo is one, Routerank another. They don't only offer airport to airport searches (or city to city if travelling by rail); they look at address to address, taking into account the amount of time it takes to get to the airport and rail station. Not only that, they give options for self-driving and public transport and come back with a full travel-time picture, so-called 'door-to-door'.

What's more, they also give filters to sort travel options by time, connections, routing, price and even CO_2 emissions. That's becoming much more important to companies, as mentioned previously, as laws around emissions are gradually becoming enforced – and policed.

The good thing for the travel manager is they can control content when employees go via their advised channels. Not only can they ensure emphasis is laid on preferred suppliers and negotiated rates, they can use behavioural economics to subtly influence travellers towards choices they want them to make. This helps control costs and keeps employees on track; they spend less time searching for travel options and more time working at their actual jobs.

Travel Risk Management 1

To be clear from the start, travel risk management isn't about scaremongering. It's to make sure that processes are in place so that should something happen, help is immediately underway, rather than finding oneself in a crisis situation without knowing what to do.

At the planning stage of the booking process, it's good practice to share information with travellers about the destination. This could range from a small briefing paper to a full report, and is very much dependent on the location and whether this is classified as low or high risk.

As discussed in chapters two and four, this information is generally maintained and shared through a third party like Anvil or GEOREACH. It's with their expertise that destinations are looked at and risks are mapped according to likelihood of occurrence and impact. And it's their information that's linked to the planning process, although it should also be possible for employees to access the information on demand regardless of whether they're planning a trip or not.

So let's have a look at a couple of examples of how this could look for someone planning a trip. Note that these are not based on real cases, but are written to exemplify the use of travel risk management.

First up, a trip from London, United Kingdom, to New York City, United States. For the example, we're only going to look at risk to personnel (rather than all the other items discussed in chapter four).

Security: Mugging / Theft

Likelihood of occurrence: medium
Impact on traveller: high

There's a medium risk in most metropolises across the globe for mugging – sadly. The impact on the individual involved in the incident is high as they could suffer from shock or could even have been physically maltreated.

Now, when travelling to New York City, mugging is probably not the first thing that comes to mind. But if you're made aware of the possibility (like it's so often done now on the subway or posters), you can take some easy precautions that don't hinder your enjoyment of the trip but might greatly contribute because you won't have an incident. That's really the aim of the information briefs shared with travellers at various stages of the trip: be prepared.

Our second example looks at a more 'out-of-the-way' location: Lagos, Nigeria. This is slightly different in so far that a traveller would have rather different associations in their mind than when travelling to New York.

Security: Kidnapping

Likelihood of occurrence: high
Impact on traveller: high

In this case you might ask yourself, 'why even go?', but there may well be good company reasons that mean you had better brush up on your self-defence skills. Joking aside, remember that travel risk management is about risk mitigation. It means the employee is well-prepared for the journey ahead and all possible care is taken to safeguard the traveller.

So in the case of Lagos, Nigeria, posters about mugging wouldn't do the traveller much good (although it doesn't hurt to have them). A better solution here is GPS fencing – the traveller can move unhindered to the locations that she needs to get to. The GPS coordinates have previously been shared and are part of the safeguarding programme. If she leaves the radius at any time, her GPS tracker kicks-off an alert to the TRM company. Firstly, contact is established with the traveller to find out whether she's deliberately 'out of bounds'. If this can't be established, a taskforce is directed to get her out. Sounds very James Bond, but that's how it is.

And that's exactly why travel risk management is so important; to be prepared when you need to be, to know what not to do in order to avoid unpleasant situations and to be secure in the knowledge that there's a backup plan should something go wrong.

Trip Authorisation

As previously mentioned, trip authorisation helps with keeping travel demand in check. It aims to probe trip plans before they're booked, to ensure company's money is spent wisely. Yet in the past, trip authorisation has also often led to frustration: travellers plan a trip, make a reservation but then have to wait for the approval – by the time approval comes, the prices have gone up and the process starts again.

However, when there's no trip authorisation in place, travellers tend to book their preferences and sometimes might be tempted to go on trips that might not be economically justified (had they been discussed with the line manager).

So when online booking tools (OBT) came on the market, one of the features soon became trip authorisation. It simplifies the process by automating messages to the line manager and even chasing them if they haven't responded within a set time limit. But not all planning (and booking) is done through the OBT. In complex cases, travel that involves multiple destinations for example, it's still down to the travel agent on the phone and the traveller to obtain approval.

But trip authorisation isn't only about cost control and managing demand. It's also another checking point to keep travellers safe while on the road.

Travel risk management needs to be part of trip authorisation to ensure the travel manager and security manager are aware of employees going to high-risk destinations. But how do they know?

Previously we discussed the risk matrix (the likelihood of something happening and the impact it would have on the traveller if it did). This matrix is used during the planning process (in the background, of course) and provides the traveller with the destination information.

When planning a trip to a high-risk location (as determined by the matrix) a secondary trip authorisation is sent out to the travel manager and the security manager. They not only need to give approval, too, but will also monitor the situation in that location closely and set up relevant alerts to ensure employee safety – even before the trip commences.

Knowing the difference:

Reservation: making a reservation means the travel agent is keeping a particular flight or hotel on hold pending confirmation. Usually, a reservation can only be held for 24 hours.

Booking: the moment the traveller confirms the reservation.

Ticketing: the time the agent confirms the booking in the system and issues the ticket (regardless of whether this is paper or virtual).

They also discuss the travel plans with their third-party travel risk management provider so everyone knows that a trip is upcoming. Depending on the destination, further briefings are necessary for the employee. These could even include workshops on how to behave in the location, what to do and what to avoid. It's also the time to talk to the traveller about GPS tracking, geo-fencing and even RFID (radio-frequency identification). While it can be put in place easily enough nowadays, it's necessary to obtain travellers' approval in this case, as there's a lot of personal data connected with any of these devices – and that shouldn't fall into the wrong hands, of course.

Finally, the security manager and travel risk management supplier will continue to closely monitor the situation in the destination prior to travel. It could be that they pull the plug on the trip because of the possibility of events that might jeopardise the safety of the traveller.

Trip approval might be a straight 'yes or no' question for trips to known and (somewhat) safe places. But it can become increasingly complex when dealing with destinations that are deemed dangerous.

Booking the Trip

Had you thought before reading all this that there were so many hoops to jump through? Well, that's why corporate travel management is needed after all. And possibly, in future it'll all be different because data can be integrated and booking outside of policy doesn't mean travellers are 'unsafe' or not taken care of anymore.

So let's look at booking the trip, after planning, reading up on travel risks at the destination and getting trip approval. We already looked at the OBT and the call centre: the OBT is great for simple 'there-and-back-again' trips to known destinations. The call-centre agent is great for complex, multi-stop trips and to provide further information on locations that the traveller visits for the first time.

Once the trip is booked, the employee receives the confirmation and the itinerary. Often this is linked to their calendar app, so travel plans immediately show on the calendar, too. Having this information handy helps with setting up meetings abroad, obtaining a visa (if necessary) and also getting to the airport on time.

For now, we've focussed on companies with a mandated programme – employees have a travel policy they must stick to and book through the corporate channels. But there are companies that take a different approach, empowering travellers by giving them tools to book travel the way they prefer. Naturally, the latter method needs to have back-office processes in place to ensure duty of care.

Empowering travellers, engaging travellers – it's happening throughout the industry. The days of 'one size fits all' are gone even in corporate travel and the smartphone is doing a fair bit to ensure personalisation comes sooner rather than later.

So how can a travel manager encourage open booking (i.e. outside corporate channels) while keeping travellers safe and knowing where they are when they travel?

Communication, as so often, is key. If the travel manager just opens the floor and tells employees to book whatever they like it's going to be mayhem. A travel policy is still needed, even if travellers are empowered! They need to know, for example, how much they can spend on a trip in order to be reimbursed for the expense. There's likely going to be rate caps for hotels depending on destinations.

Google (in this case the company and not the search engine), an early adopter of empowering travellers, has a policy in place that gives employees a certain amount of money to spend per trip. The employee can choose to use the full amount for the trip or spend less. If there's a saving, it can be used for future trips, thus making it possible for travellers to choose where to save and where to 'splurge'.

But even Google's employees need to adhere to the very simple mandate: share the itinerary. As mentioned above, once a trip is confirmed, the traveller receives confirmation and the trip itinerary. This email needs to be forwarded to one of several suppliers of capturing open-booking information (like Concur and their TripLink system). The data can be analysed and used to safeguard employees, just like booking through corporate channels would do. Or? Well, not just yet. While the data is available, there are no standard ways to fill out an itinerary. This differs by booking platform and also by supplier, thus making analysis harder.

Duty of care is also still a bit of a thorny issue, as trips aren't usually authorised when planning and booking on the web – this could mean relevant risk information isn't shared on time (or not at all). However, open booking is a field that's been hyped in 2012 and 2013, dropped off the radar for some time and is now coming back in focus. One thing's for sure, it's one to watch.

On The Go

Naturally, there's usually some time to fill with things like packing and preparing presentations or meetings before travel commences. As mentioned above, there might even be some training or briefing about the destination depending on various factors.

But now we're good to go. Travel starts and for many of the road warriors out there, they might heave a sigh of relief to finally be outside the grasp of the travel manager; free to do as they please. Or so they hope. And even as little as five years ago they would have been right.

Times are changing, however, and the smartphone has done its best to enter not only into different industries, but most importantly into our personal lives. It's unthinkable not to be connected, and if there's an issue with internet connectivity people feel anxious about missing out on something (it might be an idea to put the book aside here for a second and check your phone for emails, notifications and social media updates).

Corporate travellers are no exception and this could very well be their 'Achilles' heel'. While traditionally, people had one mobile for work and one for personal use, the trend today is much more BYOD – bring your own device. This holds true for mobile phone and, increasingly, laptops as well.

So why is this important? Well, communications, as discussed in chapter four, can make a travel programme work. On the flip side, lack of communication or too much 'spamming' can also break a travel programme and disengage travellers. Below we look at communications with travellers while on the go and give some guidance about giving just the right amount of information.

Every cloud comes with a silver lining and so does the smartphone! And in this case, the benefits might even outweigh the perceived 'nagging' of the travel manager.

First of all, you guessed it, there's travel risk management! When employees are travelling, the smartphone provides a necessary link between them and the company. We look at what happens while the employee is on the road: how do they interact with the company (or third party) when an incident occurs? But we also look at risks that might not be so obvious – unsecured Wi-Fi connections, for example.

For the traveller, another benefit might be offers that are pushed through to their phone while travelling. For example, they might partake in an airport loyalty scheme and so be notified of special sales going on as they walk through the door. Or they might get offers from the airline or hotel directly about upgrading their seat or room, tempting offers! These ancillary services provided by travel suppliers often come at a premium. But can the traveller expense these? Do they know what's in policy and what's not? And what if they could find out right there on the spot?

At the end of this 'on the go' part, we look at ad hoc purchases. Things travellers might need (like the odd bottle of water), how these decisions are made, what's possible to expense later and how travel managers might influence these on-the-spot decisions. Again, all thanks to the smartphone.

Communications

The art of communication is a much-discussed subject in academia, but also in business. It's used in marketing and advertising and, of course, in our personal lives as well. And let's not forget that communication doesn't only mean talking! It's also, and often more so, about listening and understanding information.

For travel managers, the challenge is hitting the right balance of when to push information to the traveller and when to just have it available so he can consume it at his leisure (or even not at all). It's the age-old question of what's essential!

For travellers, the challenge is to know where to find information they can 'pull' if they need it. Often this seems to be trickier than it should and employees call colleagues (and everyone else) to find out how to access certain information.

There are several important parts to successful communications: attentiveness, comprehension, user friendliness and relevance. Basically, one needs to capture the attention of the audience, communicate clearly so that everyone understands what is being said (or written), ensure that the information disseminated in the communication is easily accessible (possibly via a link) and that listeners know where to go to find out more. It should also be made relevant to the audience rather than losing oneself in details that aren't important for the key message to be heard.

Now back to our corporate traveller on the road! Information to be pushed out is, of course, that concerning the well-being of the employee. We go back to text-based messaging (still the preferred method for communications during incidents) in the travel risk management part two section below.

Information pushed out to the traveller is generally to ensure they don't spend money on things that are already paid for. For example, a traveller might opt to have breakfast in a nearby coffee shop without realising that breakfast at the hotel is actually included in the negotiated rate. Since often time has passed between booking and travelling, the traveller might be excused about forgetting what's included in the rate, especially when it's a multi-day trip visiting different locations.

In this case, push-messaging really can make a difference. Using location-based messaging, the notification could be scheduled to come in as the traveller enters the hotel and read something like 'remember that your hotel reservation includes breakfast'. Simple, yet effective.

Knowing the difference:

Push communications: information is pushed out to the employee at a time decided by the travel manager.

Pull communications: the traveller pulls information when they're in need of knowing more about a certain topic.

Adapted from push/pull marketing strategies (Marketing-made-simple.com n.d.)

Another example of using push-messaging is for transport from the airport. This could be dependent on time, so the advice would differ for travel during daylight hours ('please take the subway') and evening/night time ('please take a taxi as it's late').

And just so we're clear, this is behavioural economics applied practically. As discussed in chapter three, there are several ways to influence people and guide them to make preferred choices. Targeted push messages for corporate travellers fit the bill beautifully. If you're interested in more on this topic, have a look at the *Traveler Management Survival Guide* published by BCD Travel (2013).

So if all that information is pushed, what other information is left to be pulled? Plenty! Most importantly, possibly, is easy access to travel policy so travellers can pull information on the go.

There can be location maps, smartphone compatible of course, with the preferred hotels of the area and the company's office. Advice on what to do in an emergency. Health advice and addresses and phone numbers of doctors and hospitals. But also fun things, like restaurant tips (possibly with discount offers) and entertainment options.

There are no boundaries on what information to provide. But knowing the limitations of space on smartphones, travel managers have to make sure whatever they provide can be accessed without clogging up storage and be legible on tiny screens!

Using apps might be one way to have all information 'stored' in one place, but there's something else travel managers need to be aware of: roaming charges. We come back to this topic in the 'hidden spend' part of this chapter, but suffice it to say there's no point encouraging travellers to save money if this is subsequently spent on messaging and retrieving information.

Travel Risk Management 2

Here we are again with travel risk management. This time looking at what happens when the traveller is on the go. Already at the planning stage we looked at how travellers can prepare for risks and how they are prepared – either by their companies or third-party travel risk management provider. The latter generally only applies for travel to high-risk destinations.

But what if the traveller left his laptop in the coffee shop at the airport because he was on the phone when hearing the last boarding call? He pulled on his jacket and ran to the aircraft, only realising the laptop wasn't with him when on board and the aircraft's doors were closed. This might not sound like a terrible situation, uncomfortable for the employee, definitely, and embarrassing, possibly. But surely nothing more? But what about the information on that laptop? How secure is the encryption?

There are many laptops, tablet computers, smartphones and even good old paper files lost during travel, be it at the airport, in a hotel or on a train. Or maybe even in a park somewhere the traveller had a sandwich. The fact remains the same – there's a loss of data, opening up a security breach for the company.

This, in turn, could lead to information being released that wasn't supposed to be. It could give other companies a competitive advantage. It could cause loss of reputation. And all that is a big risk for the company – yet often it's not looked at when thinking of corporate travel.

Staying with the topic of data loss, let's look at something else that's often a sore point for employees: secure connections. As leisure travellers, we often delight in free Wi–Fi services at airports and other locations. We happily click away our lives to be able to share the latest news (and pictures) with our friends and family. And too often, we're tempted to behave this way when we're travelling for the company as well. We're only human, after all.

Using unsecured Wi-Fi can be an option if the traveller is able to connect her own VPN (virtual private network) – which ensures a safe connection for company data, like emails and files. If this can't be established (quite a few of the promotional offers won't allow a secure connection to run) the corporate traveller should not log into their emails or files because they can be read not only by the internet provider (and often by permission of the user), but also by other users using the same connection (Geier 2013).

Naturally, there are the more usual risks, like falling ill, having to evacuate a hotel because of a fire alarm or being mugged, amongst others. It's advisable for travel managers to hand out credit-card-sized information cards about what to do in case of an emergency. The information should also be on the smartphones of all travellers, of course. But there are possibly situations when the phone isn't with the person; they may have forgotten to take it from the room during the evacuation, or the battery may have died. It's good to have a paper-based hardcopy with you – and remember to hang on to at least that.

Ancillary Services

Let's now take a look at other things that might tempt the corporate traveller while on the road – things that are a headache to the travel manager because of their lack of transparency (and, therefore, comparability): ancillary services.

For the time being, let's assume the employee has gone through the company-approved channels when planning and booking their trip. They're now coming to the airport and are greeted at the check-in counter with some ancillary service offers the airline now has – more legroom (premium economy maybe, not business class just yet), lounge access (seeing as it's another two hours until departure) or priority check-in (the queues at security are dreadfully long today).

The traveller might be tempted to purchase one of these options, hoping, but not knowing, that this might be reimbursed later. Fact is that she's definitely going to try to expense it. There are many reasons (even good ones) why these offers should be paid for, and paid for by the company. So why weren't they considered during planning? One reason is that airlines have different ancillary products on offer, and until recently these weren't portrayed in the GDS.

So to get the true like-for-like comparison on a booking, the travel agent would have to go direct to all the airline websites to find out the prices for the ticket with pre-included ancillaries. That's very time-consuming. Luckily, through the NDC initiatives currently ongoing, there's hope that apple-to-apple comparisons are soon to be possible – even in the GDS. It's just a matter of time now (and, of course, of all the other things that are changing simultaneously).

And that's only the options at airline check-in. Depending on the route, it continues on flight as well with food, beverages, entertainment and Wi-Fi. Once the traveller arrives at the destination, there's more of the same with car rental (further insurance, re-fuelling by car rental company rather than do it on the way, satellite navigation, etc.) and hotels (upgrade for the room, room service, laundry service, Wi-Fi/internet) – the list is endless.

In 2012, *Business Travel News* together with some travel partners conducted research about the frequent traveller (also called road warrior). It's an insightful read, albeit slightly out of date now. The graphic on the next page shows an overview of expenses business travellers think they can claim, compared to what the company policy is. It's surprising that quite a few travellers think they can get away with a lot of ancillary offers, while they actually can't. But also, on the flip-side, how many services they believe they can't buy, when in reality a lot of companies would reimburse them (The Frequent Traveler: Finding a Balance 2012).

This, obviously, is a clear case for communications gone awry, or rather, not being applied in time. It becomes more apparent, looking at it from this angle, why accessible information is so important and why travellers should always be able to pull the exact information they need when they need it.

Expenses For Which Companies Reimburse

According to Travelers		According to Buyers
55%	Hotel room Internet access	79%
50%	First checked bag	91%
37%	Inflight meals/snacks	51%
34%	Second checked bag	40%
32%	Mobile device	63%
30%	GPS in rental car	60%
29%	Hotel premium class	10%
28%	Inflight Internet access	48%
28%	Premium car rental	10%
25%	Mobile subscription plan	40%
24%	Airline seat upgrade	27%
23%	Airline premium class	15%
20%	Airport lounge membership	12%
19%	Inflight entertainment	9%
18%	Expedited airport processing	28%
18%	Priority boarding	16%
12%	None of the above	2%

Figure 3 - BTN Frequent Traveller Report

Hidden Spend: Ad Hoc Purchases

Finally, there's ad hoc purchases. That's not to say that ancillary services aren't also often bought ad hoc, but this section looks at purchases that are made and often hidden from the view of the travel manager. And while we call them 'ad hoc' they do occur regularly, like dining, entertainment, public and other ground transportation and roaming.

Already in chapter three we discussed travel suppliers, amongst them the above group called 'hidden spend' suppliers (BCD Travel 2013). And while behavioural economics helps to influence decisions, as seen above, it's not until expense reports come in that the travel manager knows how successful it has been. And that's only if the travel manager has access to expense management data – more about how this ties in with business intelligence in chapter four.

So let's look at these ad hoc purchases during a trip. Naturally, the employee needs to eat while abroad, and not all trips are full of evening entertainment. There are generally two options (bearing in mind that it's the company which select the one for their travellers): per diem and 'pay-as-you-go'.

Per diem is a pre-allocated amount that varies by destination and is paid out to the traveller regardless of whether it has been spent in full. On the flip side, if the traveller spent more than the per diem, it's on their own bill.

BTN publishes a travel index annually, looking at hotel, car and food spend for 100 US cities, as well as Top 100 international locations. In its 2015 Index (BTN - *Business Travel News* 2015), the average food per diem amount came to $96.89, while Honolulu, Hawaii brought in the highest per diem amount of $129.25. Internationally, the average was $108 with Caracas, Venezuela, leading per diem food prices at a whopping $425.

'Pay-as-you-go' means collecting the receipts of purchases made and expensing everything once back in the office. The next part in this chapter deals in more detail with expense management.

Then there's entertainment – this could be with clients, prospects or colleagues. Care needs to be taken by the employees not to be seen as bribing someone – and extravagant entertainment could be detrimental to the company in the long run. For example, taking clients out for a meal is perfectly acceptable and possibly even considered 'good practice' after a long day of meetings. But taking a prospect to a Formula 1 race because it's known that the decision-making person is a huge fan, could be perceived as bribery. For more information on this, check out the UK's bribery act 2010 – even if you're not living in the UK but dealing with a company from UK (or a company that has offices located there) the laws apply (Ministry of Justice 2010)!

Finally, let's take another quick look at ground transportation options, including public transport. Already in chapter three we covered Uber and other ride-share options. In practice, having the Uber app on the smartphone saves the traveller time and hassle. They know where the car is, they know what kind of car to look out for (including number plate), they often have a picture of the driver (just to be sure), they know where they're going while they're going there (checking the route through the mobile app) and, lastly, they don't have to worry about having cash because everything is done through a pre-set-up account. Easy-peasy.

More hassle, but definitely cheaper is public transport. Take London as a prime example for getting around on the tube, rather than in a taxi. And, depending on the size of the city and congestion, it often takes less time to go via underground links as well.

Follow Up

You might think that once the traveller is back from her trip that's it. Maybe there are some pictures to post or order prints of, reminders of a good time. It's not the case in corporate travel, I'm afraid. There are reminders and often of a good time, too, but they're in the form of carefully collected receipts.

This collection might sit for some time before employees can muster up the strength to tackle the admin involved. But back under the watchful eye of the travel manager, that is, back in the office, there's little time to dawdle.

There are several ways to expense management, and I'm sorry for the repetition, but once again it depends on the company, and often also on the office location (because of differing country regulations).

Going back to the question of per diem or pay-as-you-go, this part explores in more detail how travellers pay for their needs on the road – and how they get the money that is owed to them.

Next to expenses there's feedback to give. Did the traveller have a pleasant trip? Yes, thank you, very much so. Naturally, the travel manager would want more detail on this.

And to round it off, we're going back to business intelligence. Not only is this important for the travel programme, but also for the actual traveller. Why? Well, because the traveller should, at the end, benefit from the travel programme – and policy.

Payments

While you could argue that payment should be part of the above 'on the go' section, it's closely linked to expenses and so it seems sensible to write about them in one go rather than jumping back and forth.

There are several payment options, but before distinguishing those, let's relook at these two:

Per Diem

An allocated amount, dependent on destination, is provided for the traveller. Per diem, as you'll know, is Latin for 'per day'; meaning if the traveller is away for three days, this allowance is paid for every day on the road. Note though, that it's customary to pay the amount after the trip.

However, there are circumstances the employee can ask for an advance, so as not to be too much out of pocket.

Pay As You Go

The traveller pays all costs on the road, collects invoices (either digitally or in hard copy) and expenses these via the company's system after the trip.

Per diem is relatively straightforward, in so far that the employee gets the allocated amount into her bank account. But there are quite a few options around pay as you go:

Personal Credit Card

A common option, especially for smaller companies, is to ask employees to use their own, personal credit cards (or other means of personal payment) for their trip costs. The traveller should be careful to ensure his card(s) works abroad and that costs incurred through foreign transaction are covered through expenses.

Company Credit Card

For medium and large companies, it's more customary to issue corporate credit cards. But beware: in many cases these are still linked to the employee's personal bank account to pay off! Travellers are still expected to do their expenses and be reimbursed thereafter.

Naturally, there are exceptions to the rule and there are companies that issue cards and pay them direct, too.

Virtual Credit Card

The trend, as discussed in chapter two, is beginning to have an impact on the industry and with good reason. Virtual credit cards are paid in full by the company and can be issued for a certain amount of time – and a capped amount of money. This makes them a safe payment alternative, especially for people travelling for a company who aren't employees – consultants, speakers and job applicants, to name but a few.

There are some other options to pay while on the road, cash or cheques come to mind, and while these might be used for the odd bottle of water or bus ticket, the future of payments seems to lie with technology (like mobiles).

Mobile wallets are also starting to have an impact as these are an easy way to pay. However, since they're connected to either a personal card (most often today) or a company card (this is a more recent development that's going to spread), they're not mentioned as a category in their own right.

Remember that the per diem amount is paid whether the traveller uses all the money or not. Meaning there's possibly some savings to be had!

This might not be interesting to the senior executive, but, to the lower ranks it can make quite the difference.

Note that it's common for airlines and hotels to be paid centrally through either the firm or the travel management company. This might also hold true for car rental, depending on the negotiated deal. So when we talk about paying for or expensing trip costs, it's what we discussed in the hidden spend section above: dining, entertainment, ground transportation and other so-called sundry costs.

Expenses

That's the payment side of things done, so let's move on to the expense process. Again, there are several ways to go about it. The advanced options use mobiles – taking pictures of receipts, while the more traditional options deal with the actual hard-copy receipts. And sometimes it's a mixture of the two.

As mentioned in the technology provider section of chapter three, there are several companies offering expense management solutions. Concur is an established brand in this space and their solutions are traveller-centric, which is just what we're looking for in this chapter.

Claiming expenses is an administrative job, often not well-liked by travellers, hence new technologies are much appreciated. The issue is that it's time-consuming. Imagine you're a frequent corporate traveller, on the road about three weeks per month. During the one week you're in the office, you have to do your job, and get the expenses done – and there are masses of them.

Now imagine you're not only travelling within one country but abroad too. Different currencies, different taxations, different receipt standards – and all those receipts stuffed in various coat pockets, wallets, briefcases and suitcases. It's a mess that's the reality for a lot of people.

The traditional process means sorting receipts and processing them into an (online) expense management tool. This means, for every receipt, the employee needs to write what it is, when it happened, who it happened with (if applicable), amounts, verifications and the budget against which to charge all of this. The hard-copy receipts are numbered as they're punched into the system and finally shipped off to the company dealing with them at the back-end.

The 'submit' button in the tool then triggers a couple of emails; to the provider (to look out for the actual receipts in the post) and to the line manager/budget holder to review the expenses online and approve, question or deny them.

Just reading this you can imagine how much time is spent on this and subsequently lost for actual work.

The new approach, and one that is gaining more acceptance and better features over time, is a virtual method to expense management. This means travellers can claim expenses while on the road. For example, having a coffee, checking emails (on the VPN, of course!) and just before leaving, taking a picture of the receipt, loading it into the app and you're done with it. Today's apps are so sophisticated (most of the time at least) that they are able to read the receipt and fill in the expense form on their own. Though while the technology is still being fine-tuned, travellers have the option to manually make changes and submit. It's no wonder travellers like this, but companies should too, as it saves them time and money (and nerves) as well.

Traveller Feedback

With the expenses out of the way, it's time to check in with the traveller about their experiences – planning, booking, on the road and even expenses should all play a part in this initiative. Because only when the travel manager knows what works and what doesn't can she take steps to make adjustments. And, as said before, if travellers feel like their feedback is taken on board, they get a sense of ownership of the travel programme, making them more likely to comply.

Obtaining traveller feedback can be easier said than done though. Employees, after all, have a job to do and might already have a plethora of emails in their inbox. A request to share information about a recent trip might simply be sidelined – not because the employee doesn't want to do it, but simply because there are not enough hours in the day. So what can travel managers do to find out what travellers think?

Surveys

Using surveys, and communicating these through various channels, is a comprehensive way to get a lot of information with only a few clicks. Distribution channels could include the weekly internal newsletter, a blurb on the company's intranet and/or social media site and, of course, in the 'welcome home' email (even though the chances are slim that many will click on the link).

The content of the survey should be structured, straight to the point and multiple choice. It's always good to offer space for opinions or ideas as well, but multiple choice is easy and, more importantly, quick to complete.

Care should be taken whether to ask about the whole travel programme or about a specific item. If it's the former, it's an idea to keep it all high-level and do specific follow-ups after the analysis of the results. If it's the latter, it's important to make the questions as specific and detailed as possible to really get all the input needed on the subject.

Pulses / Polls

A pulse is a quick survey with a maximum of three multiple–choice questions. This is great to use on the trip and even better within a mobile app. Pulses or polls can be scheduled to appear at a certain time or at a certain destination (just like notifications). After a booked chauffeur–driven transfer, for example, a poll could come up with the question 'how satisfied are you with your transfer?' and then give several answer options.

The benefit of using these short surveys is that the traveller can easily fill them in on the road. It doesn't interrupt the workflow but helps to improve the travel programme and vendor selection.

However, it's advisable to remember those dreaded roaming charges – it might be an idea to push polls through only when devices are connected to Wi–Fi.

Focus Group / Face-to-Face

Travelling is all about face–to–face interaction, though sadly, travel managers have far too little contact with travellers themselves. An idea to improve this is to piggyback on departmental meetings, 'stealing' half an hour to put a face to a name, talk a little about the efforts and reasons behind the travel programme and collect feedback on what works and what could be improved.

When collecting feedback from travellers, it's not only to ensure the right suppliers are selected or that screws can be tightened at the negotiation table. Important as that is, it's also the chance to get buy–in from travellers, simply by giving them reasons why to be compliant to policy. And that's a good time to remember that people generally want to comply, but often aren't aware that they're in the wrong (or don't understand the reasons behind a certain rule). As the workforce becomes younger, explanations and buy–in become ever more important to run a successful programme.

Business Intelligence

Traveller feedback is a great source of business intelligence, but, as you remember from chapter four, it's not the only source. Booking and transaction data, together with payment and expense information, build a more holistic view on travel spend – and also on the travel programme. So let's take a look at how business intelligence can help improve the travel programme and policy for the traveller.

Booking Data (pre-trip)

Data is considered pre-trip when a booking has been made but travel has not yet happened. In other words, changes might still be made to the booking.

This data feed is important for the travel manager to find out what travellers are initially selecting and booking. It gives her an indication of booking behaviour, whether this changes by travel destination or employee location, and how this fits with the travel policy. It also reveals the selection of suppliers and whether the ones preferred by travellers are also the ones on the preferred supplier list.

Transaction Data (post-trip)

Transaction data is collected post-trip, meaning a picture of what travel actually did happen.

A comparison to booked data gives information whether cancellations occurred on a certain route or for certain destinations. It also gives insight into which suppliers – and service levels – travellers end up using.

If resources are available, digging into those cancelled bookings might prove a worthwhile effort. Finding out what are the reasons behind these cancellations could yield valuable information to improve the programme.

Payment Data

Travel managers can obtain payment data through credit-card providers – but only if they offer corporate cards to travellers in the first place. And as seen with third-party data integration in chapter four, TMCs can help bring data sources together for the travel manager.

Payment data helps to find out what services and products travellers buy on the road. It's then easy to discover how many employees use Uber's taxi services already, for example. The travel manager then might well want to include sharing economy providers in the travel policy.

Expense Data

To an extent, expense data validates payment data. But that's only half the story – it also enriches it because it includes cash buys and more information about purchases made (as just discussed in the expense section above).

Having expense data helps travel managers find out how many employees use public transport and how many rely on flagging down a taxi. This is all valuable input to tweak and fine-tune travel policy, not only to save money but also to put in place safeguards for travellers. And, you guessed it, travel risk policy can also benefit from this data stream.

Lastly, business intelligence can be used to incentivise the travel programme or for gamification. Individual travellers or departments might benefit from such an initiative – and so will the travel manager. Running this will make sure travellers understand policy and the programme and are eager to comply – and win.

Summary

The last chapter introduces the use of life cycles in business and, more specifically, in travel. While excitement and sentiment play a large part in travel planning for the leisure traveller, the same doesn't hold true for someone travelling for business.

The life cycle of a corporate traveller is very different; the decision to travel doesn't lie with her, but rather with the company. Lead times are much shorter, too. Often travel commences within two to four weeks of booking and the destination depends again on business needs, rather than personal choice.

From the life cycle we moved to the trip life cycle, taking the emphasis away from the traveller's decision and to the travel process itself. The stages described in detail are planning and booking, on the go and follow-up. All of which describe the traveller's part to play, but also connect the dots back to the travel manager.

Planning a trip emphasises the use of corporate channels; the new technologies that help save time so employees can concentrate more on their work, rather than on the travel options. Behavioural economics is a great tool to use in the planning stage to steer traveller behaviour into preferred channels.

Another part of planning is travel risk management, which needs to be addressed at this stage for the traveller's well-being and security.

Finally, trip authorisation, that is, obtaining approval from the line manager for a certain trip and the actual booking of travel. And this completes the first phase of the trip life cycle.

While travellers on the go might think they know what they can and cannot do on a trip, there are ways to help them comply with policy. Communications, especially the use of text messages or app notifications, are a good way to remind travellers of what they already paid for during booking and what alternative options there might be to taking a taxi.

Another round of travel risk management, focusing on unsecured Wi-Fi networks and other risks travellers might encounter on the road reminds us how important the topic is. And how often it's overlooked.

Purchasing ancillary services, like extra luggage on a flight and making ad hoc buying decisions are the other items to communicate to travellers about.

The follow-up phase of the trip life cycle looks at what payment options are available to travellers today (and what is likely to be happening in this space in the future). Furthermore, the benefits of spend allowances (per diem) and reimbursements (pay as you go) are discussed.

Expenses lead into payments, so we looked at different forms of claiming these – and the tools that are currently available in the market. Note that different countries or companies might prefer hard-copy receipts and manual input, whereas the trend is clearly to go completely digital, taking pictures of receipts and submitting these on the go.

Another important part of the follow-up phase is getting traveller feedback. There are several way to obtain this: – polls, surveys or focus groups, to name but a few. The gist is to find out what works, what doesn't, which suppliers are well-liked, which are hardly booked and why.

Traveller feedback is one source for business intelligence and, together with other data, builds the backbone of the travel programme. It's this information that transforms the travel programme, making it better and more traveller-centric.

Getting travellers involved in the travel programme, even if it's only through surveys, and making changes according to their feedback results in buy-in and a sense of ownership. Travellers will want to be even more compliant when they see their ideas are being taken seriously, and when policy is explained!

That's the end of your introduction to corporate travel management; an industry hiding in plain sight. I hope you've enjoyed the journey and have deepened your understanding of business travel – and corporate travel's part in it. So let me end this book by wishing you a happy landing!

Bibliography

BCD Travel. 2013. "bcdtravel.com." *The Traveler Management Survival Guide.* Accessed January 19, 2016. www.bcdtravel.com/the-traveler-management-survival-guide/.

—. 2013. *Hidden Spend Infographic.* Accessed August 22, 2015. 1ufrwr1faezp30wik71qj4iz.wpengine.netdna-cdn.com/wp-content/uploads/2014/04/Hidden_Spend_Infographic.pdf.

—. 2013. "Traveler Management Influence." *BCD Travel.* Accessed January 12, 2016. www.bcdtravel.com/wp-traveler-mngmt_influence/.

Brassington, Franaces, and Stephen Pettitt. 2007. *Essentials of Marketing.* Harlow: Pearson Education Limited.

BTN - Business Travel News. 2015. *BTN's 2015 Corporate Travel Index.* Northstar Media. www.businesstravelnews.com/Business-Travel-Research/BTN-s-2015-Corporate-Travel-Index/.

BTN - Business Travel News. 2012. *The Frequent Traveler: Finding a Balance.* Northstar Media. www.businesstravelnews.com/Business-Travel-Research/BTN-Research-Issue-The-Frequent-Traveler.

Cook, Damian. 2014. "Slide Share Net." *Trip Advisor.* September 29. Accessed January 12, 2016. www.slideshare.net/DCookEFT/trip-advisor-39658805.

Geier, Eric. 2013. *PC World.* June 28. Accessed January 19, 2016. www.pcworld.com/article/2043095/heres-what-an-eavesdropper-sees-when-you-use-an-unsecured-wi-fi-hotspot.html.

Marketing-made-simple.com. n.d. *Marketing-made-simple.com.* Accessed January 19, 2016.

Ministry of Justice. 2010. *The Bribery Act 2010.* Ministry of Justice. www.businesstravelnews.com/Business-Travel-Research/BTN-s-2015-Corporate-Travel-Index/.

Travelport. 2010. "Sete." *The Well Connected Traveller.* Accessed January 12, 2016. sete.gr/_fileuploads/entries/Online%20library/GR/101201_Travelport_The%20Well%20Connected%20Traveller.pdf.

Glossary

Here's a list of corporate travel jargon and abbreviations to help you through the book, and possibly in real life as well.

Americas
Geographical region comprising North America (often called 'NORAM') and South America (somewhat confusingly called LATAM most often). Note that it's dependent on the company whether Mexico is counted towards north or south.

Asia Pacific (APAC)
Geographical region comprising Asia and Southwest Pacific (Australia, New Zealand). This region is also known as APAC, and there are some companies splitting Asia from Southwest Pacific as their booking behaviour and programme maturity are quite different.

Application Programming Interface (API)
This is a facilitator for different software programmes to interact. It's important in corporate travel to connect different booking sources, profile information and other (third party) content.

Association for Corporate Travel Executives (ACTE)
One of the global associations, particularly renowned for their efforts in educating the industry. They have several annual conferences across the world and many more local events and web-based trainings.

Average daily rate (ADR)
The ADR refers to either hotel or car rental rates. It's calculated by dividing the actual daily room revenue with the total number of rooms sold.

Average ticket price (ATP)
The ATP refers to air fares. It's a key metric to look at air-fare trends. Take this with a pinch of salt as it becomes distorted the larger the area is that the ATP refers to (e.g. an ATP for the route of London–New York in economy class is very helpful because it's specific; a global ATP holds almost no value as too many variables are thrown into one pot.

Best available rate (BAR)

The BAR refers to the best non-negotiated rate on the day at the point of booking. This can include special rates that have to be pre-paid.

Blackout dates

These are dates during which hotels are not bound by the negotiated rates – provided they have been shared during the negotiations. For example, if the city hosts a big conference, hotels might apply blackout dates as demand will be high.

Business Travel News (BTN)

One of the media publications focusing on business and corporate travel. They're especially famous for the Corporate Travel Index and Fortune 100 company lists they publish annually.

Buying Business Travel

Another media outlet focusing mainly on the UK market and hosting great debate events together with ACTE (see below).

Corporate rates

Rates that companies negotiate together with the supplier; note that every company has their own corporate rates with suppliers.

Corporate social responsibility (CSR)

Corporations are increasingly urged to take on social responsibility. Often this is done through engagements with the local community. In corporate travel, CO_2 tracking and supporting projects or charities to combat emissions are one way to show responsibility.

Corporate travel management (CTM)

The managing of corporate travel, encompassing day-to-day operations, negotiations, duty of care and travel risk management on behalf of a company. Often in-house travel managers (see below) are supported by external travel management companies (see below).

Data consolidation

Within corporate travel, data consolidation refers to bringing different data sources together. These are usually booking and transaction data, supplier data and also payment and expense data; all of which is used for business intelligence and informed decision-making.

Distribution channel

This is the process of how the suppliers get their products to the travellers. The traditional distribution channel for corporate travel is the global distribution system (see below), though there are online alternatives through brokers as well as direct.

Dynamic pricing

In corporate travel, dynamic pricing offers an alternative to negotiated rates (especially for hotels). Prices are driven by the market and by demand, so they can vary from low in off-peak season to high when all rooms in a city are needed (for example, during a congress).

EMEA

Geographical region comprising Europe, Middle East and Africa. There's a shift in the industry to separate Europe from Middle East and Africa as the latter two are becoming more important economically – this is likely to continue, meaning Middle East and Africa will become distinct regions as well.

Expense management system

An all-important tool for travellers to be reimbursed after travel, the expense management system offers a range of features, including reporting, approving and paying expenses on an online platform.

Geo-coding

This is the ability to use coordinates, that is, degrees of latitude and longitude, for finding specific locations. It's also becoming increasingly popular with hotels to match property names and addresses for billing and reporting purposes.

Geo-fencing

Geo-fencing refers to the ability to track travellers in high-risk destinations. By using GPS signals (mostly), an alarm is raised when the traveller moves outside of predefined areas.

Global Business Travel Association (GBTA)

The other global association helping the corporate travel industry grow. Their members are travel managers and suppliers, sharing opinions and information to find best processes for the industry.

Global Distribution System (GDS)

There are several GDSs available around the world that connect supplier inventory with booking agents. Amadeus is particularly well-established in Europe, while Sabre has a stronghold in North America. Travelport is an important GDS in Asia.

Hub

An airport offering long-distance (often international) flights and many short-distance 'feeder' services is called a hub.

International Air Transport Association (IATA)

An important body, not only for corporate, but for all travel, IATA establishes standard practices and is also the governing body for international air-travel rules. Furthermore, they accredit travel agents, making the agency able to book through the GDSs and collect commissions for their bookings.

IMEX

A Frankfurt-based convention for meeting suppliers, featuring a hosted-buyer programme. Individuals and companies arranging meetings are invited free of charge to attend (including travel arrangements). In return, they have to schedule meetings with suppliers and other exhibitors.

Institute of Travel and Meetings (ITM)

This is one of the local associations operating in the UK Similarly to their global counterparts, they put on a range of localised events for travel managers and suppliers to exchange information and learn about the industry.

Itinerary

A chronological record of a traveller's trip, including all information about booked services, like flight information, hotel, car-rental and any other pre-booked items.

Key performance indicator (KPI)

Travel managers set targets for the travel programme and monitor these by using key performance indicators. They often include advance booking time, economy class ratio and online booking behaviour as well as many more programme-specific ones.

Lowest logical airfare

Corporate travellers are advised to use lowest logical airfares, and what is considered logical is determined by travel policy. For example, there might be cheaper flight options, though due to stopover connections, these might not be 'logical' for the company.

Managed travel

This means travel is actively and professionally managed within a corporation. It generally also means travel policy is in place and rates are negotiated with suppliers.

MICE

An industry abbreviation for meetings, incentives, conferences and exhibitions (or events in some cases).

Negotiated rate

This term is especially important for bookings on the GDS, as the client's code is needed to access negotiated rates agreed upon with the supplier.

Online booking tool (OBT)

As the name suggests, this is a tool for travellers (or their admin/agent) to use for booking travel. It's often customised for big corporations and gives the traveller access to preferred suppliers and rates. Using an OBT is time-efficient and costs less money compared to calling an agent on the phone (which is why this is an important KPI to track).

Online Travel Agency (OTA)

In the corporate travel industry, online travel agencies are completely virtual and don't have walk-in services.

Per diem

A daily allowance for a city or country that the corporate traveller receives when travelling.

Preferred suppliers

These are the suppliers that corporations have negotiated deals with. Hence travel managers try to drive business to these products and services.

Pre-trip authorisation

A process prior to booking to obtain approval, usually from the line-manager, for the trip.

Profiles

In corporate travel this refers to profiles stored within a customised database in the GDS. These profiles contain traveller information, preferences and loyalty cards and mean traveller data is automatically copied into a booking.

Rack rate

The rate hotels publish for their room. This is often the highest rate available and is usually displayed at reception.

Red-eye flight

A term for late-night flight departures, arriving at the destination early in the morning. The term is most commonly used in North America for west- to east-coast travel.

Request for information (RFI)

Before the travel manager decides which suppliers to invite to bid for their business, he often sends out a request for information first, to be able to compare suppliers' services.

Request for proposal (RFP)

Once a general selection is made about which suppliers to invite, a request for proposal is sent out. This is a document asking detailed questions about products, services, duty of care, price and other items, and determines whether a supplier is going to become the preferred one with a company.

Revenue management

Also known as yield management, this is the practice of suppliers (mainly airlines, hotels and car-rental companies) of controlling inventory and supply to maximise occupancy and revenue.

Service level agreement (SLA)

Similar to KPIs, these measure the quality of services and make sure key suppliers are adhering to them. Assessment factors are, amongst others, response time to answer phone calls, policy enforcement and contract savings.

Skift

An online publication offering global travel-industry intelligence. While they're looking at travel overall, they often have interesting thought pieces on corporate travel as well.

Tnooz

Another publication focusing on technology in travel. They're often looking at the future and what's going to impact corporate travel.

Travel Management Company (TMC)

An intermediary company to support corporations with managing their travel programme. They traditionally book travel, like agencies, but also look after the many back-office needs of corporate travel, like duty of care requirements, negotiations, payments and many more.

Travel manager

The person in charge of travel management at a company. This might be a single individual or a full team, depending on the size of the company.

Travel risk management

An essential part of travel management is managing risks on the road as well. This is often done using a third-party (specialist) provider.

Unmanaged travel

A term used for companies that don't travel enough to require a travel programme or policy in place. They often don't have negotiated deals in place and many book through online channels only.

Value added tax (VAT)

A tax imposed by many governments across the world on goods and services. This tax is often recoverable for corporations – even across borders.

World Travel and Tourism Council (WTTC)

An international organisation of travel-industry executives promoting travel and tourism worldwide. Its members come from the global business community as well as from governments.

World Travel Organization (UNWTO)

An organisation formed by the United Nations to promote responsible, sustainable and universally accessible tourism.

Key Word Index

36766508R00113

Made in the USA
San Bernardino, CA
01 August 2016